-PRESENTS-

So the Bastard Broke Your Heart,

NOW WHAT?

— PRESENTS —

So the Bastard Broke Your Heart,

NOW WHAT?

TASHA CUNNINGHAM,
founder of DontDateHimGirl.com

Avon, Massachusetts

The Polka Dot Press® name and logo design are registered trademarks of F+W Media, Inc.

Published by Polka Dot Press, an imprint of Adams Media, a division of F+W Media, Inc.
57 Littlefield Street, Avon, MA 02322. U.S.A.
www.adamsmedia.com

ISBN 10: 1-60550-682-6
ISBN 13: 978-1-60550-682-1

Printed in the United States of America.

10 9 8 7 6 5 4 3 2 1

Library of Congress Cataloging-in-Publication Data
is available from the publisher.

This publication is designed to provide accurate and authoritative information with regard to the subject matter covered. It is sold with the understanding that the publisher is not engaged in rendering legal, accounting, or other professional advice. If legal advice or other expert assistance is required, the services of a competent professional person should be sought.
—From a *Declaration of Principles* jointly adopted by a Committee of the American Bar Association and a Committee of Publishers and Associations

Many of the designations used by manufacturers and sellers to distinguish their products are claimed as trademarks. Where those designations appear in this book and Adams Media was aware of a trademark claim, the designations have been printed with initial capital letters.

The stories used throughout this book are true but names have been changed to protect privacy.

This book is available at quantity discounts for bulk purchases.
For information, call 1-800-289-0963.

CONTENTS

ACKNOWLEDGMENTS

This book is dedicated to every woman who has ever had her heart broken by a guy. Think of this book as your new best girlfriend, supporting you every step of the way during your bad breakup. This book is also dedicated to my husband, an outstanding man to whom I'm honored and humbled to be married. I love you with all my heart! You are truly the love of my life! I hope every woman who reads this book finds a wonderful, honest, loving man like you!

I'd like to give a huge thank-you to everyone at the William Morris Agency, including literary agents Mel Berger and Eric Lupfer. My heartfelt thanks go to Chelsea King and Laura Daly at Adams Media. Thank you both for sharing my vision for this project and guiding me throughout the process. Thank you to my friend Mary Martin for her inspiration and wonderful support on this project. I'd also like to thank my mom, all my fabulous girlfriends, and every woman who's ever logged on to *www.DontDateHimGirl.com*!

Proceeds from your purchase of this book today will be donated to the DDHG Empowers Fund.

The fund provides microgrants to charitable organizations around the world to support women's programs and initiatives. To learn more, please visit *www.DontDateHimGirl.com /EmpowersFund*.

INTRODUCTION

One day in 2005, a girlfriend of mine, reeling from the aftermath of yet another bad breakup, shared her story with me. She had been cheated on, lied to, and used by a guy for over a year. She couldn't understand why she kept dating the same mediocre lineup of cheaters, liars, and losers over and over again. I, like many of you, knew the feeling. My dating resume was dismal. What was *my* problem? I always took them back and allowed them one more opportunity to break my heart.

My girlfriend and I were addicted to bad boyfriends and we just couldn't break the habit. Over and over again, we found ourselves smack in the middle of a bad relationship with a guy who wasn't close to boyfriend-worthy. Somehow, we ignored the signs that we had a cheater, liar, or loser on our hands. One day I wanted to know exactly how many undateable guys I'd gotten involved with that year. I was doing something wrong in the way I dated and I wanted to figure out what it was. So, I made a list. I wrote down the names of my last five boyfriends and five things I didn't like about each one. I called it my "Don't Date Him, Girl" List. It was going to be the one thing that would remind me not to date yet another loser. I carried it with me everywhere I went and consulted it like an oracle every time I met a guy that seemed even remotely boyfriend caliber. So, I made a list. I wrote down the names of my last five boyfriends and five things I didn't like about each one. I called it my "Don't Date Him, Girl" List. It was going to be the one thing that would remind me not to date yet another loser. I carried it with me everywhere I went and consulted it like an oracle every time I met a guy that seemed even remotely boyfriend caliber. My Don't Date Him, Girl list was my secret weapon. It was like a roadmap that helped me navigate the sometimes bumpy road to true love. On page 21, I'll show you step by step how to create your own Don't Date Him, Girl list so the next time you meet a guy you'll be prepared to spot warning signs and old dating patterns.

Then, I took Don't Date Him, Girl online and created DontDateHimGirl.com (DDHG), a little place in cyberspace where women (mostly my girlfriends and I, at first) could blog about the guys they dated and talk about what went wrong and what they learned from the experience. I envisioned that one woman's bad experience could save another woman some heartache down the road and that a network of support could be built around the site.

Things didn't go quite according to plan, however. I underestimated how much men would hate the site and how vocal they'd be about it. When a story about the site hit the front page of my local newspaper, I knew DontDateHimGirl.com wasn't going to stay tiny for long. Practically overnight, my little site became a thriving social networking community of women from all over the world—more than a million of them—who have experienced good and bad dating relationships and want to share those specific experiences with other women. Suddenly, everyone was talking about DontDateHimGirl.com and as the site's creator, I found myself in the center of the storm.

On DDHG, women can post a guy's name and offer information other women might find helpful if they want to date the same guy. Guys who are talked about on the site can log on and share their thoughts as well. We also have hundreds of great, informative articles by contributors on everything from how to spot a guy who will cheat to how to boost your self-esteem. DontDateHimGirl.com touched off a controversial battle of the sexes that continues to this day. Soon after that local newspaper article, a media frenzy that I couldn't control was ignited and I found myself in places I never thought I'd ever be—shaking hands with Ann Curry on *The Today Show* set, fielding questions from CNN's Jeanne Moos via satellite, on the cover of newspapers and magazines, and on the radio and TV, talking about DontDateHimGirl.com. The *New York Times*, CNN, MSNBC, *GQ*, and countless other media outlets wanted to find out about it, and for months so it went.

While women were ecstatic and found DDHG empowering, men were outraged. Although women can post about both good and bad dating experiences on the site, those men who were called out for their allegedly bad dating behavior online weren't very happy about it. I understand where those men are coming from. So I created features on the site to help it do what it was indeed to do—create a spirited dialogue about dating and relationships that would help women date safer and smarter. I created a feature that allows anyone to contact the author of a post via e-mail through a link at the top of every post. The database of posts is no longer available to the general public logging on to the site. Users must now log-in to their password-protected accounts on DontDateHimGirl.com in order to gain access to the database. But I also understand the women who visit DontDateHimGirl.com. I've talked to many of them, read their stories on the site, and helped them with their dating dilemmas. Most are bad-boyfriend addicts who have been victims of cheaters, liars, and losers. They want to talk about it and help other women avoid it in the future. By the time a woman finds DontDateHimGirl.com, she is so caught up in a vicious dating cycle that she's never stopped long enough to figure out why she can't break her bad-boyfriend habit. Most women have never examined how they got into the bad relationships they've had. Again and again, they let losers into their love lives with disastrous consequences.

On the flip side, most men who visit the site have never stopped long enough to figure out why they cheat on, lie to, and deceive the women they date. They're caught up in a cycle of their own. On DDHG, we help both sexes find answers. DDHG dating experts personally help hundreds of men and women untangle their difficult dating dilemmas with innovative, out-of-the-box dating advice. DDHG doesn't bother giving you advice on how to change yourself so a man will marry you; we take the focus off "your future husband" and put it squarely where it belongs—on you and what you're going to need to heal your broken heart. That's exactly what you'll find in this book. I'll show you how you got into this situation in the first place, give you a ten-step plan to get your brokenhearted butt in gear, show you how to create and use your Don't Date Him, Girl list and make better decisions about the men you date. We'll also talk about what to do (and what *not* to do) while you wait for Mr. Right. As you read, you'll discover some unique ways to recover from your relationship woes. You'll meet women just like you who've been through exactly what you're going through right now. Each story has one thing in common—every single woman found a way to get her broken-hearted butt in gear and get back on the dating scene in search of love. I'll share some of my own dating foibles and tell you how I finally found the man of my dreams. Surprisingly, I found true love because of DontDateHimGirl.com.

To give you perspective, you'll get advice from dating experts like author Alison James and Atlanta-based licensed professional counselor Sonia Torretto—both women who have been exactly where you are right now, too. You'll also get an inside look at exactly how guys think when they're dating, courtesy of advice from reformed cheaters, liars, and losers, including DontDateHimGirl.com resident expert on all things male, The Average Guy. He's a former flagrant philanderer who now tells women how they can avoid dating guys like the one he used to be.

With each page you read, you'll take comfort in one very important thing—you're not alone in what you're going through. Millions of women around the world battle bad-boyfriend addictions and hideous breakups every day. And when they do, many turn to DontDateHimGirl.com to get advice, share their stories, and meet other women who have gone through similar experiences. These are the compelling stories of women just like you, with hearts just as broken as yours.

Whether you were cheated on, lied to, or otherwise hurt by a guy, you're in good company. Dating disasters like that have happened to the best of us over and over again. Some of the smartest women in the world have been duped or swindled by men who appeared, at first, to be pretty close to perfect. Let's learn from our mistakes once and for all.

The good guys *are* out there—so leave the losers in the dust and find them!

PART 1

DAMAGE CONTROL

So a Bastard Broke Your Heart, Now What?

Picking Up the Pieces

You've been dumped. You're miserable and probably furious too. How are you going to handle it? The same old way you usually do—crying, obsessing, and maybe even plotting revenge against your ex? You've been doing that routine so long that it's time to ask yourself whether it's really working for you. Chances are it's not. You suffer during the breakup, then you allow yourself to *continue* suffering in its aftermath! It's time to break the cycle and move on in a healthy way.

Unfortunately, the situation is not going away on its own. You have to deal with the aftermath of this nasty breakup. You have to push through the pain of losing the guy you probably thought was the love of your life. He was your dream guy— someone you were *sure* you'd spend the rest of your life with. Sadly, what you dreamed of wasn't meant to be. You weren't meant to wear his ring or walk down the aisle with him at your wedding. For whatever reason, you were meant to go your separate ways. He's not coming back and you're not going to try to get him to return, either. No, ma'am! You're going to spend your time getting your brokenhearted butt in gear, healing, and finding love again—this time, with a guy who is truly worth it.

But it hurts, you say. Of course, it does! Bad breakups are never pleasant and they wreak havoc on a girl's emotions. Breaking up is like a pap smear—extremely uncomfortable. But the good news is one day soon, the bastard who broke your heart will be a distant memory. You survived that discomfort and you'll survive this breakup, too! Now it's time to get over him—*really* get over him—for good.

Brokenhearted Syndrome—The Scientific Facts

You'll be happy to note that the broken heart you're sporting at the moment is actually a scientifically recognized ailment. It's a malady known as Broken Heart Syndrome, or as doctors call it, stress cardiomyopathy. Every minute of every day, a woman somewhere in the world becomes afflicted with it. What causes it? An experience that breaks your heart—for example, the loss of a loved one, a spouse's infidelity, or a mate's sudden, pronounced, emotional withdrawal from your marriage or relationship. The symptoms simulate those of a heart attack: chest pain, shortness of breath, low blood pressure, and even congestive heart failure!

It's fitting that the symptoms of Broken Heart Syndrome mirror those of a heart attack, because if you think about it, when you break up with a guy, your heart does get attacked. Your poor heart was just doing what it does best, loving someone, then bam! It was beaten, stomped on, and crushed. To make matters worse, the attacker is a man you once loved. Heck, you may still love him at this very moment despite what he's done to you.

The bad news: Doctors don't prescribe cupcakes, cosmos, and chocolate to cure Broken Heart Syndrome. The good news: You have the power to cure your ailment. I'll show you how in this book.

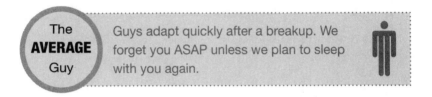

The **AVERAGE** Guy

Guys adapt quickly after a breakup. We forget you ASAP unless we plan to sleep with you again.

But it's up to you whether you use this breakup as an opportunity to make real change in your love life or you let your broken heart hold you back from finding happiness.

Your Mission

I think you're ready to make a change in the way you date. Otherwise, why are you in the bookstore looking for some good postbreakup assistance? You want to stop dating the same cheaters, liars, and losers over and over again. I know you do. You want to heal your broken heart. It's been shattered too many times and it's finally time to put it back together again. You want to find love again one day. I promise, you can do it, no matter how sad or pathetic you feel right now.

Whether you've been cheated on, lied to, dumped, or had to do the dumping yourself, you've got one mission in life at the moment: to nurse that broken heart of yours back to health. Then, you can create your Don't Date Him, Girl list and quickly audition brand-new boyfriends worthy of your time.

The AVERAGE Guy	If you've been dumped by a guy, he was over you way before he ever told you he wanted to breakup with you.

It would be much easier to morph into a miserable, moping couch potato and only leave your house for two reasons:

1. To purchase fattening vanilla ice cream hoping to relieve the painful symptoms of this breakup or
2. To kill your pain with tasty cosmos courtesy of the cute bartender at your neighborhood bar.

After all, what's better than getting over a guy armed with a carton of vanilla ice cream and a delectable cosmo assembled by a really hot bartender? Not much! But now isn't the time to give in to your temptations. Now is the time to take control of your dating destiny, instead of letting some guy do it for you, like you usually do. It's time to learn from your past dating mistakes and make a real commitment—not to a guy, but to yourself and to your heart this time.

This Breakup Too Shall Pass

You probably think you're going to feel bad forever. You think you'll never, ever be happy again, all because of what your ex did to you. But guess what? You're wrong! Like your ex, the aftermath of this breakup will be just a bad memory.

It's not going to take forever, but resuscitating your broken heart will take a little time. Breaking your bad-boyfriend addiction isn't going to happen overnight. Kicking the habit is a process that occurs little by little, day by day. How much time is this healing thing going to take, you ask? How long before you stop believing you'll never find a decent guy to give your heart to? How long before the nightmare of this breakup ends? The answer depends on you!

As it stands right now, you've got two choices. You can:

1. Let this breakup beat you, turning you into a sulking spinster for eternity. In that case you might as well just close this book right now! Do it quick, before time runs out! You've got to get to the grocery store before all the vanilla ice cream is gone!
2. Take the advice offered by DontDateHimGirl.com's dating experts and the many women who will share their stories with you. If you do, you'll discover that you, too, can put the pieces of your broken heart back together. It isn't impossible!

So which path will you choose? Why not banish the pain your ex caused you, move past it, and find love again, instead of gaining weight from the vanilla ice cream and sustaining liver damage from the vodka? Whatever you choose, one thing is certain—one way or another, the guy you're sulking about right now is going to be the last entry on your Don't Date Him, Girl list because you'll never date a cheater, liar, or loser again. But for now, it's going to hurt. One way or another, this breakup too shall pass. How long before it does is entirely up to you. In the meantime, here are some effective strategies for dealing with your pain.

What *Not* to Do

First and foremost, don't overdose on vanilla ice cream and vodka, please! You'll still be miserable when the last spoonful or sip hits your lips, not to mention how terrible you'll feel when both hit your thighs. Instead, put the spoon down and realize that it's okay if you still love him. There's nothing wrong with you. You're not just going to go from loving him one minute to hating him the next, no matter what he did to you. Emotions just don't work that way. They take time to grow and they take time to die, too. Here are some ways to stay off the emotional roller coaster.

STOP TRYING TO "FIGURE HIM OUT"

Right now, you want to know why he did what he did. You want to know why he screwed his coworker or why he couldn't curb his penchant for strip clubs, texting his ex, or lying to you about doing both. Anyone can understand your need to know. But ask yourself—does it really matter now? Will you ever know what *really* happened?

Women spend *way* too much time after a bad breakup running through mock scenarios of what went down in the relationship when they weren't looking. Some women become fixated on knowing every detail of their lover's transgressions instead of becoming obsessed with their own personal well-being and healing their hearts after the breakup.

The truth is, whether you are engaged, married, or just dating when a breakup strikes, wondering why he broke your heart is a waste of your precious time. Stop speculating, assuming, and drawing conclusions about what he was thinking or doing when the two of you were together. Are you ever going to know the truth? Nope! Your questions aren't going to get answered, so let it go. Who's going to tell you the truth—your ex (who lied to you)? The girl he cheated on you with? Why would she help you? Don't count on it, girl!

Unfortunately, when a guy breaks your heart, the Goddess of Truth doesn't magically appear bearing the answers you so badly seek. So, you're never really going to know what happened. Accept that. Nothing you can do is going to change it. Stop and take a few minutes to let that sink in if you need to—but don't let your quest for "the truth" hold you back from healing your broken heart.

If you really think about it, you'll understand why you don't need to know about your ex's dastardly deeds. You already have a pretty good idea of what he *might* have been doing. You may even know *exactly* what he did. In either case, there's no need to confirm it or dwell on it. He isn't; why should you?!

AVOID THE BLAME GAME

In almost any parting of ways between lovers, the question of who's at fault rears its ugly head, demanding to be answered. When it does, don't you dare play the "Who's to Blame" game! Contrary to what your ex has to say about it, you are not the only one to blame for this breakup. He's played a prominent role in it, too. You probably bear some responsibility for what happened, but just how much is open to interpretation. And the answer you'll get depends on which ex you ask. Unfortunately, a single girl reeling from a bad breakup can spend a lot of her precious time assigning blame for the demise of a dead romantic relationship. Don't bother, girl!

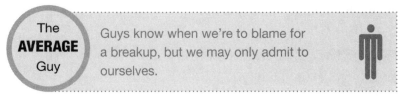

The **AVERAGE** Guy

Guys know when we're to blame for a breakup, but we may only admit to ourselves.

None of that matters now anyway. What matters is that you're going to commit right this second to healing your broken heart and moving past this awful breakup so you can embrace a new, fabulous love life that awaits you just around the corner. You've just got to learn a few things about men and dating and the various effects that come with them before you get there.

DON'T BEAT YOURSELF UP

Right now, you're probably convinced that you're the unluckiest brokenhearted girl in the world, banished by the love gods to live out the rest of your days single, sad, and solo. Oh, please! Stop being such a drama queen! No woman in a relationship is immune from the pain of heartbreak. Whether you're a famous actress, the wife of a wealthy politician, or the married soccer mom down the street, your heart can be broken by a guy at any time if you're in a romantic relationship. You, your mother, your sister, your best friend, Cleopatra, Jennifer Aniston, Hillary Clinton, Christie Brinkley, and millions of everyday women around the world have all had their hearts trounced by a guy once or twice.

Suffering a breakup is hell on a single girl's self-esteem. Beating yourself up over this breakup isn't productive for your head or your heart. Don't give in to the temptation to feel sorry for yourself, question your sexiness, or doubt your desirability.

Instead, ask yourself this question: Are you really going to kick and scream and sulk your way through this breakup? Or are you going to keep reading this book and avoid becoming a bitter bitch prone to wrinkles, Botox, bad boyfriends, and yet another breakup somewhere along the line?

STOP THINKING THAT YOU'RE BROKEN

There's one thing you've got to know about the nasty business of breaking up right upfront: just because he broke up with you doesn't mean you're broken. Because you've been broken up with, you take it as a blaring sign that somehow, you're broken and need to be fixed. You think there's something wrong with you just because some guy saw fit to break your heart. Rest assured, honey, there's nothing wrong with you. You're simply a product of your dating environment. If you've always dated cheaters, liars, and losers, you're going to have battered self-esteem, make bad dating decisions, and have great difficulty breaking the bad-boyfriend cycle you're in.

Don't worry. It happens to the best of us. I've been exactly where you are right now—lost, alone, and hopeless about my dating future. I've questioned my intelligence after falling for a jerk and kicked myself for letting a con artist Casanova dupe me. I blamed myself for every bad breakup. But after a while, I got smart about the guys I dated and so will you!

What You *Should* Do Right Now

Now that you know what *not* to do, here are some actions you can take to put yourself in the right frame of mind to get over your latest loser.

It's not easy forgetting about the guy who broke your heart. If you were together for a long time, it's going to be even harder to banish the memories. But there are ways to help you curb thoughts of your former flame. C'mon, you can do it. It's not as difficult as you think it is. Here are three great ways to start.

....

3 WAYS to Banish the Memories of a Bad Boyfriend

1. **Delete your ex from your life.** Remove his phone number from your cell phone. Delete his e-mail address from your list of contacts and get rid of copies of the lovey-dovey e-mails he sent you during the course of your relationship. If these things are gone, you won't be tempted to waste your precious time rereading his old e-mail declarations of eternal love, and you won't face the danger of getting sentimental and then trying to contact your ex. This will just begin your bad-boyfriend cycle all over again.

2. **Stop following him.** Stop looking for your ex at his favorite places. Don't stop by his favorite bar because you know you stand a good chance of running into him there. Who cares where he goes now? Monitoring your ex's comings

and goings should be the last thing on your list of things to do. Stop visiting the places you two went together. Ditch the coffee run to the Starbucks where he told he loved you for the first time. Don't bother to go back to that little Italian restaurant he took you to last Valentine's Day. And while you're at it, find another gym, because the one you went to when you joined together is off limits now.

3. **Stop giving him a recurring role in your love life.** First, don't talk *to* him. Even if he calls you dozens of times, don't answer. You're broken up and unless you have a child together, there's not much you really have to say to him now. Second, stop talking *about* him. When you talk about an ex, you give him power to control what you're doing in the present, which makes no sense since you're not together. Stop talking about him every chance you get to anyone who will listen. Sure, you're going to talk about exes from time to time, but don't make a habit of mentioning him every time you have the opportunity. He's not an important part of your life anymore. Instead of talking about him, talk about your new goals and the things you plan to achieve in the future. Soon you'll see that if you stop talking about him, you'll forget about him.

LOVE YOURSELF

Resolve to love yourself more than you love the guy who broke your heart. That's right. You've been playing second fiddle to your boyfriends for way too long. It's time to make yourself number one for a change. Your priority now isn't him; it's you! Too often, women put themselves last on the list of things that are important in life. You do it, too, whether you realize it or not. In your last relationship, did you ever find yourself being too compromising or too willing to overlook your guy's obvious flaws? Were you too willing to give up control of your heart to some guy? Yes, I bet you did, but that's okay. You have to make mistakes in order to learn. The good news is you'll never make the same dating mistakes again now that you've got this book in your hand!

As you read this, you may still feel bad about your *breakup*, but the key is not to feel bad about *yourself*. Going through your life feeling like you're not worthy of love, that you did something wrong, or that your breakup was your fault is not productive, because when you feel bad about yourself, you don't make good choices. There are bad guys out there who prey on women who feel bad about themselves and suffer from low self-esteem. And by walking around with your head hung low because of this breakup, you're just making it easier for a bad guy like that to prey on you or kick you while you're down emotionally.

Part of getting over a broken heart is getting your self-esteem and confidence back on track. What do you have to feel bad about, anyway? You're finally free to fulfill your true dating destiny with a great guy, not continue wasting your precious time with more cheaters, liars, and losers. You should be celebrating, not sulking!

If you're letting this breakup so severely affect your self-esteem that you've taken to sequestering yourself inside your house or apartment for days on end, you're giving your ex complete control over your emotions and the way you're going to deal with this breakup. Think about that. You're not even together anymore and he still has some say in how you feel and what you do. Ridiculous!

Do you think he's living on his couch, eating himself into oblivion, and missing you? Nope! And you shouldn't be either. There's a whole world of decent, eligible guys out there and you won't find them by sitting in your living room staring at the TV every night, feeling bad because of a breakup. Don't sit around hoping, wishing, and praying that you'll reconcile with your ex or that you were taller, skinnier, or prettier. You're already perfect just the way you are, so stop waiting for your ex to come crawling back or wishing you were something that you aren't just to please him. Instead, move yourself forward and find a new guy to love—one who is actually worthy of your time.

LEARN THE TRUTH ABOUT MEN

To help you heal faster, let me tell you a few key things you need to know about guys. You may not have known these things in the past, but armed with this information, you'll make better dating decisions about the guys you let in your life.

They Obsess about Sex

Did you know that every fifty-two seconds a man, your ex included, has a sexual thought? This may come as a big surprise to you (or maybe not!), but whether it's positions, porno, or places to do the deed, guys are thinking about sex literally every minute of the day! In case you're counting, that's more than 1,000 times every twenty-four hours. With all that sex on the brain, it's no wonder guys have little room up there to ponder the important things in life, like marriage, kids, and buying you all the fabulous shoes and purses your heart desires.

They're Afraid of Commitment

Guys in relationships tend to get sick, but not with a cold or a touch of the flu. They are allergic to commitment, monogamy, marriage, and gainful employment. We'll talk more about how to spot commitment-phobes on page 168.

They're Not Bulletproof

Every guy you meet, including your ex, has insecurities, fears, and doubts, just like you do. While most guys would like you to think they're tough and that little affects them emotionally, nothing could be further from the truth. Guys worry about how they look, what they wear, and what women think of them. They seek approval from a significant other and worry about it when they don't get it.

GET SOME PERSPECTIVE

If you've dated a loser, don't feel bad about it. Don't beat yourself up over it. It's okay. Despite what you may be thinking, you're a smart, sexy young lady who's simply had lousy luck in landing good guys. That's nothing to get upset about. Those relationships are over and those men should be out of your life. Sitting around feeling like a loser after you've taken a long, hard look at your disastrous dating history isn't going to really accomplish much, is it? You've done what *many* women before you have done—dated a few men who were cheaters, liars, and losers.

The world is overrun by bad breakups, separations, and nasty divorces. If there were a sure-fire way to avoid those things, women would probably have learned it by now, but there isn't.

There are only things you can do to make your chances of being successful at love greater.

FOCUS ON THE POSITIVE

You may feel like a failure because you're staring down the barrel of singledom once again, obsessing about the negative results of your breakup. Stop! You now have the perfect chance to start over. How do you banish those feelings of failure that creep up when a guy breaks your heart? Here are six tricks.

....

6 WAYS to Banish Bad Breakup Feelings

1. **Realize that whatever happened, it's for the best, even though you may not believe it.** You now have a chance to take your life in an entirely new direction. Perhaps you're not prepared right this second to embark on it, but you're a quick study and you'll be on the road to a new love life in no time.

2. **Understand that you're now free to roam about the dating world.** It's an exciting time in your life. You're no longer shackled by the misdeeds of your former flame. Whatever he's done doesn't matter. Your love life is completely in your control and now that you've discovered this book, you'll be much better prepared to find a great guy when you go out looking this time.

3. **Rejoice in the fact that it's finally over.** He may have told you that you were the one with all the issues, but in reality he, too, played a part in the demise of your relationship. Sure, you had to deal with the aftermath of his infidelity or

lies, but isn't it comforting knowing that it's finally over and you now have your entire life ahead of you, free of your ex's issues, problems, bad habits, and annoying behavior? It's finally time for you to exhale, and that doesn't feel bad; it feels fabulous!

4. **Hang with your girlfriends.** Commiserate with your girls at a spa day or all-girl lunch. They'll remind you of how much better off you are without him.

5. **Be kind to yourself.** Don't get down on yourself for the little things in life that don't get done as quickly as they might have had you not had this traumatic breakup thrown into your lap. A breakup is a loss, just like a death in the family or getting laid off from your job. You need time to heal before you can get back on your feet emotionally. Give yourself that time.

6. **Try an activity that you never engaged in with your ex.** For instance, just because your ex lived on his couch doesn't mean you have to be a slouch! Enroll in a kickboxing class. You never know what hot hunks may be hanging out there.

Remember: Breakups Don't *Have* to Be Bad

Have you ever wondered why most of your breakups have been so bad? I used to wonder that, too, until I realized that no one ever taught me (or any of the guys I ever dated) how to break up with someone the right way. Even if your ex cheated on you, lied to you, or deceived you, your breakup still doesn't have to be a nightmare. Here's why.

When a guy breaks your heart, it's natural to harbor resentment and ill will toward him. But think about it. Wouldn't you rather see your ex for the jerk he is and waste no time in moving on from him? The "success" of a breakup really depends on how you deal. And the way you deal with it usually depends on how you view your sudden singlehood. Right now, you're sad, scared, and sexless, but that's to be expected after a breakup. But you won't stay that way for long.

One positive way to look at it is to associate the end of your last relationship with the beginning of your newfound freedom. Your relationship may be over, but you're finally free of a bad relationship that has been holding you back.

It's liberating, actually. You may not see it this way now, but this breakup is an opportunity to break your bad habits and find true happiness in a relationship. It's going to hurt for a while, but that's okay. You're a brave, strong girl and you'll be just fine in the end.

What Your Future Has in Store for You

Think of dating again like finding the perfect pair of stilettos. You've got to try on tons of them before you find the pair that fits. That takes patience, planning, and persistence—the same virtues you'll need to get over your ex, dust yourself off, and live to love another day. Think of each guy you meet from here on out as a pair of shoes you might commit to buying one day. For the time being, though, you're going to try on a few other pairs before you decide which one you simply can't live without.

You're probably not just going to stumble upon a pair of luscious Christian Louboutins or Jimmy Choos in just the right size at just the right price. Every girl knows it takes real work. You have to scour the stores and surf cyberspace to snag a deal that will make your girlfriends green with envy. Would you stop shopping forever just because a few boutiques didn't have the shoes you wanted? No way! So why would you stop looking for love just because some bastard broke your heart once?

Jumping into the Unknown

Now that you've taken the first step in breaking the bad-boyfriend habit—recognizing that you have one—it's time to take the next step. You need to focus on curing your bad-boyfriend addiction and breaking the habit. Don't stray from that goal. It's easy to go back to the way you used to date and fall for the same unworthy guys—at least when you were exhibiting the same stupid dating behavior over and over again, you knew what to expect.

But if you change things now and break your bad-boyfriend habit for good, you have no idea what's going to happen, right? You don't know what the future holds for you if you head in another direction with your love life. Don't be afraid. There's nothing to fear. Your romantic future rests totally in your hands. Before you know it, you're going to get over the bastard who broke your heart, recover with flying colors, and find a great guy to share your love with. But this time, you'll do it without the emotional baggage you usually carry from one relationship to the next. You won't try to pin your past romantic failures on any guys you date in the future. You won't punish them for the way some other jerk treated you, either. Instead, you'll focus on the moment at hand, enjoy your date, and maybe even make a lasting love connection.

The Secret Weapon: Your Don't Date Him, Girl List

In this battle of the bad breakup, you've got a secret weapon that's going to help you get through it—your Don't Date Him, Girl list. It's easy to create your list.

1. On one side of a piece of paper, write down the names of your last five boyfriends.
2. Next to each name, write down five things you couldn't stand about each one. It could be an annoying habit he had, or something awful he did. (Write neatly because you're going to have to refer to this list often when you get back out on the dating scene at the end of this book.)

Do you see a pattern emerging? Did each guy cheat or lie? Did each of your exes have jobs? Did you lend each of them money that they never paid back? Once you've completed your list, you'll see your bad dating habits up close and personal. You'll never let another loser into your life again if you're armed with your Don't Date Him, Girl list!

Now fold up your list nice and neat and tuck it away in your purse. Refer to it every time you want to romanticize one of your exes and you need a reality check. Refer to it when you're out on the dating scene and you meet a guy that seems boyfriend-worthy. Your Don't Date Him, Girl list and this book are your new best girlfriends and with them, you'll get over this bad breakup before you know it! At DDHG.com, we've made it even easier to create your own list! Download your very own Don't Date Him, Girl list free by logging on to DontDateHimGirl.com. All you've got to do is fill it in. You're welcome!

Learn to Love Yourself Before You Love Another

Feeling Like You Don't Deserve Love

Going through bad relationships can make you feel like true love doesn't exist. There are women who believe that true love can't exist because they've been hurt so many times before. Take Rose, thirty-two, for example.

"After one bad breakup in particular, I made a promise to myself that I would never go back on the dating scene again because all the guys were total jerks," says Rose. "I had already gotten my heart broken by so many jerks that I couldn't help but think it was me, not them, and I felt really bad about myself."

But Rose found out that she wasn't the one with the problem. "I saw my ex at a restaurant after not seeing him for over a year," she says. "I had heard he had gotten married, so I introduced myself to the woman sitting next to him at the table." It turns out the woman sitting next to him wasn't his wife. "He was there with his mistress and it was then that I realized that my ex would never change. I wasn't the one who was unworthy of a good relationship, it was him." Thankfully, when Rose stopped feeling bad about herself, she opened her heart to finding love again.

"I just stopped looking at myself as unworthy every time I didn't click with a guy," Rose says. "I've got my flaws, but they aren't so great that no guy would ever want me. Besides, no one is perfect. Realizing that made me change the way I thought about myself."

Like Rose, you must stop looking at yourself as a person who shouldn't receive love and start believing you're a person who absolutely deserves to be the love of a great guy's life. Why not you? You're just as worthy of love as the next woman and don't you forget it, honey!

But you're probably where Rose was before she saw her ex—you're feeling down about yourself. Let's look at how you feel and why.

....

3 REASONS You *Think* You Don't Deserve Love Right Now (And Why You're *So* Wrong!)

1. **If your ex didn't want you, who will?** Your self-esteem is fragile right now because you are down in the dumps over this breakup. You may think no other guy will want you because your ex didn't, but you're so wrong! Not every guy you meet is going to be like your ex. From here on out, the guys you meet will see you for the amazing person that you are!

2. **If only you were different.** You may be thinking that if you changed the things your ex said he didn't like about you, you would still be with him in a happy relationship today. Let's get real here, honey—you and I both know that's

nonsense. A romantic relationship is not about changing a person to make him into what you want. It's about realizing who a person is and deciding whether or not you can accept that.

3. **If only you were smarter.** You're not stupid and you know it, so don't waste your precious time believing that you don't deserve love because you've made a few bad dating decisions in your life. So what? You were never taught how to date smart, but after reading this book, you'll have a PhD in dating the right way!

Self-Esteem Problems

It's a sad fact: Most women suffer self-esteem problems. It doesn't matter if you're in a relationship or single, rich or poor, younger or older—low self-esteem can bring you down. We're women, we're insecure, and we're constantly trying to please everyone else in our lives—our man, our boss, or our kids. But believe it or not, you have absolutely no reason to have low self-esteem. It doesn't matter what's going on in your life or what kinds of problems you're dealing with in addition to this breakup. If you have problems, they can be solved. Your problems are no reflection on your self-worth. You are good enough to do anything you set your mind to achieving.

According to the Self-Esteem Institute in Portland, Oregon, low self-esteem is a disorder prevalent among millions of women in the United States alone, not to mention the rest of the world. The institute defines it as "a thinking disorder in which an individual views himself as inadequate, unworthy, unlovable, and/or incompetent. Once formed, this negative view of self permeates every thought, producing faulty assumptions, and ongoing self-defeating behavior."

Even women who seem like they should have very high self-esteem don't always have it. A rich Hollywood actress like Jennifer Aniston seems like she shouldn't have a care in the world, but when she was enduring the horrible press surrounding her breakup from Brad Pitt, you can bet she had her moments where her self-esteem took a nosedive. She was even brave enough to talk about it honestly. But did Jennifer let that breakup hold her back? Despite the negative tabloid stories, the bad press, and the constant speculation about her relationship with Pitt, she simply plowed along, kept making movies, weathering the storm, and in the end, she came out on top. What about the humiliation singer Rihanna endured at the hands of former boyfriend Chris Brown? She didn't let it get her down. She took time away from the spotlight to heal and emerged stronger, smarter, and healthier emotionally.

You've got to do the same thing. Think of your breakup as a problem you've got. It's easily solved when you move on and take charge of your love life again. So why do women let low self-esteem sabotage their love lives?

"One reason could be that women don't believe they deserve a man with good qualities," says Sonia Torretto, professional counselor and author of *Men Should Come with Warning Labels.* "We seek out what we see in ourselves, so if we see ourselves as deserving of all those great qualities, it is more likely that we will find someone of the same."

Why Do You Have Low Self-Esteem?

Women dealing with breakups often suffer from sagging self-esteem and a profound lack of belief in themselves or love. There are many reasons women don't feel catwalk-confident every time they leave the house and even more reasons they don't believe in love. Here are some of the most common.

THAT'S HOW YOU WERE RAISED

Who's to blame for your lack of confidence? Believe it or not, the root of it could be your parents. According to the Self-Esteem Institute, parenting style and whether or not a woman has been abused either physically or sexually plays a major factor in her self-esteem and how it's formed. If your parents always put you down or devalued you in some way, those negative vibes are going to stick with you in your adulthood. In fact, you're going to be dealing with the effects of their behavior for the rest of your life. If you think your parents may have contributed to your current self-esteem problems, consider finding a good therapist to help you work through this pain.

A BAD BOYFRIEND PUT YOU DOWN

Have you ever dated a guy determined to put a dent in your delicate self-esteem by calling you names, criticizing you, or otherwise putting you down? Verbal abuse in relationships is real. I, like millions of other women, have experienced it. I was in a relationship for years with a guy whose hurtful remarks, cutting criticisms, and verbal assaults convinced me that I was worthless and that's the way I deserved to be treated by any man I dated. It wasn't until I finally had the courage to break up with him that I realized just how much I had let my self-esteem be sabotaged. In retrospect, I see now that I dated guys who had problems long before they started dating me.

Verbal abuse is prevalent on both sides of the gender fence. According to a 2006 Harris poll based on the results of the 2005 U.S. Census data of approximately 223 million adults, male and female, aged eighteen and over, 31 percent said they had been called names or verbally abused in a relationship. Social media and technology are also being used to digitally hurl insults and threats in romantic relationships. A 2009 DDHG.com poll of more than 1,300 men and women revealed that a whopping 37 percent of respondents had been abused, called names, or harassed by a significant other via text message, IM, and sites like Facebook and MySpace.

YOU'VE BEEN COMPARING YOURSELF TO FAKE BEAUTY

The mass media definitely has an influence on women's self-esteem problems. Millions of women look with envy at the retouched photos of picture-perfect models that grace the many fashion magazines on the market today. Yet most of those buxom beauties got that way through surgical enhancement, not Mother Nature. They needed the help of a scalpel and several thousand dollars to look the way they do. Only they know if it's really worth it. And then there's the thriving porn industry, which has guys convinced that all women should look like the actresses on the DVD cover, whose flaws have been miraculously airbrushed away.

Real women don't have the luxury of Photoshop to make their perceived flaws disappear instantly. Yet they beat themselves up because they don't fit the unrealistic, deceptive standards set by the males in our society of what a woman should look like.

Are You Insecure? An Exercise

How do you know if you've got a problem with self-esteem and insecurity? Take this short quiz and find out!

1. **Your boyfriend of six months buys you a sexy new dress.** You spy the tag and it's a medium and not a small. Do you:

    (a) burst into tears on the spot because you think he's secretly sending you a message that you're fat
    (b) curse him out for practically calling you a beached whale
    (c) thank him for the lovely gift and make a point of wearing the dress on your next date

2. **Your new boyfriend mentions that he's still friends with his ex.** Do you:

    (a) freak out and tell him how totally inappropriate that is and that he's got to change that if he wants to date you
    (b) compliment him on the fact that his breakup must not have been so bad if he's still friends with an ex
    (c) try to find out his ex's name so you can call her and ask about him

3. Your boyfriend is half an hour late picking you up and doesn't call. Do you:

(a) start calling him incessantly to find out where he is in case he's with another woman

(b) assume he is with another woman and start sending him nasty text messages

(c) chill out and wait until he calls you so you can tell him how worried you were about him

Let's find out how you did. In the first scenario, if you answered (a) or (b), it's clear you've got insecurity issues. Are you not happy with your body? If so, that might be why you would be so offended if your boyfriend bought you a dress that was the wrong size. He's not sending you a secret signal that he thinks you're fat. He probably didn't even look at the tag on the dress anyway because a guy buying women's clothes is like a gynecologist performing dental work—he is totally out of his league. The best thing to do in a scenario like this is (c) to graciously accept the gift, then later ask for the receipt so you can take it back and get the right size. Then wear the sexy dress out when you have your next date. In Scenario 2, if you answered (a) or (c), insecurity is the name of the game in your book. You've got it bad and you've got to get rid of it. I'll show you how to do it in a minute. If you date a guy who tells you that he's friends with an ex, don't worry about it right away. There are two things that might be going on: he may be stringing his ex along in hopes of a reconciliation and that's why they're still friends, or he could have genuinely had a healthy breakup that made it possible for his ex not to hate him and that's why they're still friends. If it's the former, you'll find out soon enough. But if you're on a date and he drops that tidbit of info, don't panic. Go with (b) and compliment him on the fact that he can actually be friends with an ex after a breakup.

In Scenario 3, if you answered (a) or (b), your insecurity knows no bounds. Your guy may be half an hour late picking you up (which is horrible), but before you jump to conclusions, find out what happened. If it's a first-time offense, give him the benefit of the doubt and don't assume he was up to no good. Instead, try (c) and wait until he calls you and let him know how worried you were about him.

If you've got an insecurity problem, now is the time to get some help.

> The **AVERAGE** Guy
>
> Guys can sense a girl's insecurity right away and when we do, we run for the door.

It's Time to Win Back Your Self-Esteem

Regardless of the source of your self-esteem deficit, it's about time you win it back and ditch any doubt you've ever had that true love isn't in the cards for you. Yes, you—the woman whose romantic resume may include several bad breakups, a couple of messy divorces, and maybe even a broken engagement or two. Even you over there, with the disastrous dating credentials, deserve to have sky-high self-esteem, a strong belief in true love, and a long-lasting romantic relationship with a great, gorgeous guy. And don't you ever doubt it!

So how exactly does a single girl win back her self-esteem? Good question! Here are three strength-building exercises for your self-esteem that will help you reclaim the confidence you've lost.

....

3 ACTIONS You Can Take to Improve Your Self-Esteem

1. **Don't let the media mess with your mind.** Have you ever opened a fashion magazine and felt bad about yourself because you didn't look like the women who graced its pages? I have, and it isn't a good feeling. Remember, those images aren't real. There are no perfect women, except in the world of software programs like Photoshop where, with just a few clicks of a mouse, anyone can be perfect. Don't let the images of retouched women that you see in magazines and movies make you doubt your own beauty, intelligence, and talent.

2. **Give up the ghost.** Many women are haunted by the ghosts of their bad boyfriends past. Long after the relationship is over, you still have horrible flashbacks of the guy who called you fat or the one who told you how great you'd look if only you had bigger boobs. You kicked these guys out of your life a long time ago, so what are their ghosts still doing stuck in your head? Kick them out of there, girl!

3. **Say it like you mean it.** Too often, women like us tend to want to please. Even if we don't want to, say, take our guy's clothes to the dry cleaner or hang out with his mom for a day as a favor, we do it. Believe it or not, this under-mines your self-esteem. If a guy you're dating, or anyone

for that matter, asks you to do something that you don't want to do or can't do because you'll be inconvenienced, say no. And say it like you mean it! It's all part of taking control of your life and putting yourself first.

PRACTICE VALUING YOURSELF

Another key step in the process of resuscitating self-esteem that is on life support is learning to value yourself. But after you've been bruised or battered in a few bad relationships, learning to value yourself can be difficult. Women tend to put themselves last on their priority list, after work, kids, school, and finding Mr. Right or dating Mr. Not Right at All. Valuing yourself means putting *you* first. It means making sure the things you want and need are your top priority. Sacrificing the things you want devalues your self-worth (you're saying what you want isn't important and thus you are not important either), and the consequences of that mindset can be dire. Devaluing yourself also turns you into a walking target for a cheater, liar, or loser just waiting to break your heart, take your money, or cause you harm.

Here are six ways to make sure you value yourself.

....

6 WAYS to Value Yourself Every Day

1. **Recite a power phrase.** This is a phrase that you say every day to affirm that you are a valuable person. Try saying something as simple as "I am valuable, strong, and productive." Say this out loud once a day, every day.

2. **Compliment yourself.** When you look good, you know it. When you've done a good job, you know it, too. Tell

yourself how pretty you are, what a great day you're going to have, or how talented you are. If you do this long enough, soon it's going to stick and instead of getting down on yourself all the time, you'll look at yourself in a whole new, confident light.

3. **Look at yourself in the mirror.** A lot of women are actually afraid to look in the mirror and take a long, hard look at what they see. I know I was. I would use my reflection solely to put on my makeup, not to analyze the inner me. But I'm glad I finally did. I looked at what I saw and realized that I should really be celebrating my reflection in the mirror every day, instead of looking for and pointing out all my flaws and putting myself down for them. No one is perfect, but many women don't realize that. Keep in mind that in each wrinkle, blemish, extra pound, or gray hair you see, you're growing, taking life's journey, and making the most of it. Don't chastise the person you see in the mirror every morning: celebrate her!

4. **Set yourself up.** Set goals for yourself in any area of your life and work to achieve them. Set good goals that will have a positive impact on your life, such as losing weight if you need to (the healthy way, please) or going back to school. Things like getting revenge on your ex for breaking your heart or spying on his new girlfriend are not-so-good goals that will definitely have a negative impact on your life. To make your goals easier to achieve, set a deadline to reach them—for example, losing ten pounds in a month or going back to school for the spring semester. If you have to, break your goals up into smaller, more manageable mini-goals. This will make what you're trying to

achieve seem much less daunting. Measure your success by what you've achieved. Once you reach what you set out to achieve, reward yourself. Go out and get yourself something nice. By achieving your goals and rewarding yourself for them, you'll be reminded of just how valuable you really are.

5. **Laugh at yourself.** When you make silly mistakes like tripping and falling in your stilettos in front of a hot guy, don't get angry—laugh at yourself instead. Silly things like that don't matter and have no effect on your value as a person. Once you can laugh at your own foibles, you'll realize that.

6. **Give yourself a little credit.** Beating yourself up over something you've done wrong isn't healthy. It only diminishes your value as a person in your eyes. Instead, be kind to yourself. Realize that everyone make mistakes, has bad days, and endures a bad breakup or two. "Women need to realize that if a guy did something bad that leads to a breakup, it's not about her," says the Average Guy. "It's about *his* insecurities, *his* fear, and *his* emotional issues. It's not about his girlfriend, wife, or mistress." You don't need to take every breakup personally.

How I Found My Self-Esteem

It happened to me. After drowning in a turbulent sea of bad boyfriends, my self-esteem was nearly nonexistent. My moment of clarity came after a particularly bad breakup where the guy I was dating was cheating on me and had helped himself to my bank account without permission. It hit me like a ton of bricks. It wasn't the guy's fault, because he was that rare combo of a cheater, liar, *and* loser. It was my fault for thinking so little of myself that I let a guy like that into my life. I did it to myself.

That's when I realized that I was the one in control of my dating destiny and the only way I was going to succeed was by placing a high value on myself and my self-esteem. I finally got smart and made me, myself, and I the top priority in my life instead of giving that spot to some guy, and I got stronger and so did my self-esteem. I learned to value myself, and soon, my love life took a turn for the better. I started attracting better guys and left the jerks behind. Eventually, I found the man of my dreams and married him. If a former perpetual loser-in-love like me can do it, you can, too! Here's what you can do to get yourself there.

CREATE AN ALTER EGO

To curb those nagging feelings of insecurity when you're re-entering on the dating scene, create a badass alter ego and bring her out on your dates. What's an alter ego? She's a character that you can play to act as if you have self-esteem.

Why Do You Need an Alter Ego?

For many women, having self-esteem is so foreign a concept that *pretending* you have it is a good way to ease into *actually* having it. Your alter ego will help you boost your chances at finding true love by building your self-confidence. She dresses with style, she holds her head high, and she is proud of herself. She is fierce! You can practice having self-confidence using her character, then gradually use her less and less when you build your own *real* self-confidence.

Take Beyoncé's Word for It

The expert in fierce alter egos is Grammy Award–winning singer and actress Beyoncé. She knows all about it! She's been quoted as saying that when she's about to give one of her fabulous live performances, she becomes another woman by the name of Sasha Fierce—her sassy alter ego who emerges when she performs onstage.

"Sasha Fierce is the fun, more sensual, more aggressive, more outspoken side and more glamorous side that comes out when I'm working and when I'm on the stage," she told Fox News in 2008. Beyoncé even paid homage to Ms. Fierce in 2008 with her chart-topping album, *I Am Sasha Fierce*.

The 3-Step Process

Take a cue from the sultry singer and create a confident alter ego for yourself. Bring her out when you're about to go on a date. When you're out on the dating scene, become her. You may not be oozing confidence right now, but she will. Follow these steps:

1. **Give her a badass name.** Beyoncé calls her alter ego Sasha. What are you going to call yours? Don't give her a boring, matronly name, like Josephine Crabtree. Instead, pick something with a little panache, like Brandy Badass.

2. **Buy her a new outfit or arrange one from clothing you already have.** Your new dating alter ego is a confident, stylish dresser. When you go out on a date, imagine how she would dress. If your usual style is jeans and a T-shirt but you know your confident alter ego would wear a sexy

black dress, don't you dare show up on a date sporting faded Levi's!

3. **Practice acting like she acts.** She holds her head up and walks proud, and she doesn't apologize for past failed relationships, because she's not even thinking about them. She's too busy thinking about her fabulous future, and you should be, too.

Mastering the art of walking around with dazzling self-confidence isn't easy. Confidence doesn't come naturally to most women, but it does come naturally to your dating alter ego, and that's why you need her!

What female walks around feeling fierce after a breakup, anyway, you ask? Not too many! You are going to start a trend. Here you are in the midst of a bad breakup and you'll still feel like you're on top of the world. You're well on your way to emerging from it smarter, stronger, and sexier.

GIVE YOURSELF SOME TOUGH LOVE

Ask yourself this: Are you really going to sit there and get down on yourself because some guy hurt you? Do you really think he cheated on you, lied to you, or dumped you because you're unworthy of his love? No way, sister! C'mon! You know better than that!

The bastard who broke your heart did those things to you because he's a jerk—plain and simple. Whatever his reason, it wasn't because you weren't worthy of his love. So pick yourself up and dust yourself off, because you've got work to do! Though it's important to be kind to yourself, sometimes you also need to give yourself a good boot in the behind to shake yourself out of your wallowing ways. Stop focusing on him and start giving yourself the attention and credit you need and deserve.

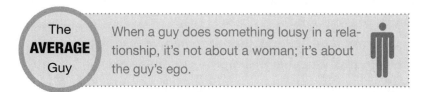

The AVERAGE Guy When a guy does something lousy in a relationship, it's not about a woman; it's about the guy's ego.

It's absolutely essential to get your self-esteem straight before you can heal your broken heart and strut your way onto the dating scene with confidence again. You are worthy of so much more than you are giving yourself credit for right now. You deserve both the love you have for yourself and the love of a good man!

Don't Give Up on Love

You're probably wondering whether true love exists at all right now. The good news: it does! The bad news: it usually doesn't arrive in perfect form exactly when you want it. While no one can be entirely sure of what true love is, we know what it isn't. It isn't a fairy tale where you go riding off into the sunset on the back of a white horse with your arms wrapped tightly around your perfect prince. Love just doesn't work out so nice and neat like that. Most of the time, love is complicated, messy, and rarely works out the way we plan for it to.

It's also harrowing and harmonious all at once. It's a gamble, a roll of the dice, a bet you make on your future happiness, hoping the odds work out in your favor.

Remember that though you want to keep searching for your prince, there are no guarantees in life or love. You may do everything right in your next relationship and it still may not work out. And if it doesn't, that's okay. After reading this book, you'll be better equipped to handle the relationship and the aftermath of the breakup. If you find yourself facing the end of another relationship, relax. Once it's over, you're going to get up, dust yourself off, and try again. That's the nature of your dating life—if at first you don't succeed, try, try again!

TAKE IT FROM THE EXPERTS

But with all the bad breakups, separations, and divorces that happen in the world every day, it's understandable that many people find it hard to believe that true love exists. Is it really something that two people can attain for even a little while, let alone a lifetime?

"If true love didn't exist," says dating expert Sonia Torretto, "then no one would bother dating again and again." Think of childbirth. If we didn't forget how bad it hurt, we would never do it again. Plus, when you find that really special guy, it makes all the pain you've gone through with guys before worth it."

In 2008, CNN.com published a story about a group of scientists at Stony Brook University in New York who scanned the brains of couples who had been together for twenty years and compared them to the brains of couples who were newly in love. An impressive 10 percent of the couples who were married for two decades had the same chemical reactions as the new couples when shown pictures of their significant others. This proves that love can, indeed, last a lifetime, debunking the widespread belief that the first stages of romantic love fade away after just fifteen months and that after a decade, any romantic feelings between a couple completely disappear.

True love is out there. . . . That's why it's so important to get back on the dating scene to try to find it!

See? True love does exist and you can fall into it. But you won't get there by walking around bitter about your bad break-ups and broken hearts. You won't get it by lounging on your couch, hoping the perfect catch will just walk through your front door. If love were only so easy, everyone would fall in it. Sadly, there are women, like Jenna, twenty-eight, who didn't believe in true love at all.

"There was a time, after a really bad breakup, I didn't believe in love at all anymore," says Jenna. "I just couldn't believe that there was a guy out there who was capable of loving and respecting me. It seemed like all of the ones I liked eventually broke my heart."

Jenna didn't believe in love and it adversely affected her ability to date. "I didn't even want to try because I just knew that every guy who paid any attention to me only wanted to get me into bed." Those kinds of guys are indeed bastards. Things changed for Jenna when she realized that she had two choices. She could either give up on love and risk living a lonely miserable life or educate herself more about how to date better and get out there and try again. "I didn't want to give my last breakup any power over my dating future," says Jenna. "So I decided to take a look at the things I was doing wrong, fix them, and then put myself out there again—but this time, avoiding the jerks that lurk on the dating scene."

Giving up on love is a sure-fire way to sulk yourself all the way to spinsterhood. When you get there, you'll weep and wallow because of the wrinkles that line your face. Sounds great, huh? Giving up on love is simply not an option, young lady! Jenna found love and so will you.

Need a little motivation? Memorize these seven reasons a single girl should never give up on love.

....

7 REASONS to Keep Believing in Love

1. **You know for a fact love exists.** You've seen and felt it so you know how wonderful it can be. Don't give up now and miss what love has in store for you!

2. **Love doesn't just land in your lap; it takes work.** You won't find love sitting on your sofa.

3. **Love isn't an exact science.** Just because you fall in love with a guy doesn't mean he's the guy you should spend the rest of your life with. Don't give up until you find *that* guy.

4. **If you give up on love, you might never know what it truly feels like.** You may think you've been in love already, but wait till you experience love with a nice guy! You don't want to give up before you do that.

5. **Girls who give up on love are prone to wrinkles from all the sulking, complaining, and wallowing they put their faces through.** Is it really worth it?

6. **If you start acting pathetic, guys will sense it.** And you know what that means—a very empty dance card for you.

7. **Giving up on love really means giving up on your future happiness.** Whether you eventually want to be married, dating, or just over the bastard who broke your heart, you won't get there if you throw in the towel now.

So don't give up. Don't settle. And whatever you do, don't feel bad about the breakup you're going through right now. You need to spend that time healing your broken heart, not mourning your bad breakup.

Don't Give Up on Finding the Good Guys, Either

You might think they're all cheaters, liars, and losers who only want one thing from a woman—sex. If you feel like that now, you're not alone. There are millions of women who share your misguided opinion. Just because you've been through your fair share of bad breakups doesn't mean all guys you meet are going to be just like the guy who broke up with you. Nothing could be further from the truth, girl! You probably won't believe this, but there are so many good guys out there. There are so many guys who are kind, faithful, and honest.

MY OWN STORY

I should know. Despite all the jerks I dated in the past, I found a man who is all that and so much more. Every morning when I wake up, I wonder how on earth I, a former dismal dater, got so lucky. DontDateHimGirl.com is the reason I found my true love. In 2005, as the media frenzy began, a story about the site hit the front page of my local newspaper. There, next to the article, was a picture of me. No big deal, right? Little did I know on that same day, the man of my dreams was also reading the paper. A few days later a good friend of mine called me and said he knew a guy who was interested in dating me. I was floored! But in the back of my mind, a question one of my girlfriends asked me surfaced. *What guy would want date the girl who created DontDateHimGirl.com?* Because I didn't realize how DDHG would take the world by storm in a tidal wave of curiosity and controversy, I was worried that I would never find love. I was convinced no guy would want to date me for fear they might end up on the site if we broke up. But I got lucky. I found the one guy who had no fear of ending up on DDHG because he was decent, caring, honest, and honorable. But I didn't know that then, so I had my doubts.

After much prodding, my dear friend convinced me to go out on a lunch date with the man who saw my picture in the paper. He took me out on December 26, 2005, and we've been together ever since. Nine months later, we were married.

But before I met him, I was just like most women out there, facing the exact same predicaments. I dated guys who cheated on me, lied to me, hit me, borrowed money from me and never even attempted to pay it back. I even went on a date with a guy who lied about his age and the fact that he had a kid. Then I dated a guy who, when he was unemployed, decided that when I was at work was the perfect time to hit the streets in search of other women.

But I don't really blame them. Yes, they were jerks, but I did it to myself. I was a horrible dater because my self-esteem was miniscule at best. I couldn't even find it at all after a while, and instead of getting help like many women, I chose to ignore it.

I also wanted desperately not to go through the same turbulent relationship scenarios that I'd seen growing up. I wanted my romantic life to be different. When I was a girl, I assumed all women went through trials and tribulations with a man at some point (or, in some cases, *many* times) in a relationship. I thought all women got cheated on, lied to, or deceived by some guy some time in their lives.

Everywhere I went I met other women just like me—women who had been abused, cheated on, lied to, and deceived by men. These women were from all walks of life—lawyers, doctors, secretaries, public relations executives—all dealing with the aftermath of the consequences of their bad relationship decisions. I wasn't alone. Really smart, savvy women who had successful careers were dating cheaters, liars, and losers. How could *they* make bad relationship decisions?

Then I reached my personal breaking point and realized it wasn't the guys I was dating, it was me. I was to blame because I sat back and let those bad relationships happen. Like many women, I ignored the signs of trouble or that a guy wasn't who he appeared to be.

Because of what I had been through, I wanted to give up on guys. I was convinced I just wasn't any good at relationships. I thought that all guys were cheating jerks. But then I met my husband—the most honest and outstanding man I've ever met. He's the guy I always wanted to be with but never thought I was worthy of having in my life. When I met him, I was reeling from the aftermath of a bad breakup after a broken engagement. I immediately realized that there were indeed wonderful, caring men in the world and I was lucky enough to have found one of them.

DON'T SECOND-GUESS YOURSELF

Many women with a track record of failed relationships begin to stop trusting themselves to have the good judgment to find a decent guy. After all, they haven't had any luck with guys before then—why would their luck change in the future? Helen, twenty-six, thought that after what she had been through in relationships, she was in no way qualified to make a good decision when it came to guys.

"I saw my dad abuse my mom," says Helen. "After so many years of seeing him do that, I just thought that's how guys were. When I got older and started dating, the only guys I attracted were cheaters, liars, and losers, just like my dad."

But eventually, like me, through therapy and lots of work on her self-esteem, Helen finally realized that she was a great person worthy of love and began trusting her judgment again. "Once I changed the way I looked at myself and my relationships with men, I was able to see that I was really a great person and that just because I'd been through a bad breakup or two, I wasn't about to give up on love or on guys." Even though she'd made mistakes in the past, Helen was just acting on what she knew to be true at the time—guys can be bastards. But she made a commitment to improving her outlook so that she could consciously find the good guys.

THINK OF IT THE OTHER WAY AROUND

If you're still telling yourself that all guys are jerks, try thinking of it this way: Convincing yourself there aren't any good guys on the dating scene is like a guy thinking that all women are gold-digging whores. While it's a fact there are indeed many gold diggers lurking, there are just as many outstanding women who wouldn't dream of dating guys with the sole intention of taking their money.

"There's one thing a woman on the dating scene has to remember whenever she gets a little discouraged," says the

Average Guy. "There's an ass for every seat and in time, she'll find the perfect one for her." Well said, Average Guy! You've also got to remember that the love of your life is definitely out there. If you're not with him, it isn't because he doesn't exist. It's because you haven't found him yet. Somewhere out in the world is a guy you can trust, admire, and love. With a little help, you're going to find him. When you do, get ready! You're going to have the time of your life with your soul mate and best friend.

Be Optimistic—but Be Realistic

In your search for that perfect guy, you don't want to settle. But at the same time, you're going to have to be realistic. Yes, almost every woman out there would like to wrap her arms around Brad Pitt, Blair Underwood, or Mario Lopez every night, but alas, often that scenario isn't in the cards.

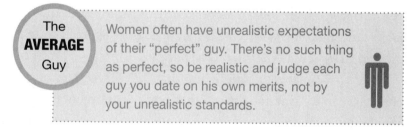

The **AVERAGE** Guy

Women often have unrealistic expectations of their "perfect" guy. There's no such thing as perfect, so be realistic and judge each guy you date on his own merits, not by your unrealistic standards.

The fact is it doesn't really matter, because you know that looks will fade over time. What's important in the next guy you choose is not the condition of his six-pack or the size of his manhood. Nope, what's really important is what kind of person he is when you're in a relationship with him—whether the chips are down or everything's going great and you're both flying high. What matters is whether or not you can trust him, honor him, and love him. Is he worth that? Is he a guy that deserves that? These are all questions you've got ask yourself the next time you get involved with a guy. Ask yourself these questions early on rather than a few years into your relationship, when you may have ignored the signs that the guy you thought was your sweetheart really isn't the one for you.

Adjust Your Dating Attitude

Not all the guys you date are going to be gorgeous hunks with hefty bank balances, but who needs that when the most important things in a relationship are love and trust? Set your expectations reasonably. You want a guy who is employed, pays his bills on time, and can take care of himself, but he doesn't have to be Donald Trump. You also want a guy you're attracted to, but he doesn't have to be a carbon copy of Brad Pitt to qualify to go out on a date with you. Madeline, thirty-four, thought she had to have it all in order to be happy.

"My mother always taught me that I deserved the best," says Madeline. "She taught me that one of my main goals in life should be to find a very rich, very handsome guy to have babies with." But Madeline soon realized how unrealistic that really was. "I did meet a great guy," says Madeline, "and he wasn't exactly the type of guy my mother was looking for, but I recognized that although he didn't have much money when I met him, he had potential and more importantly, I fell in love with him." Today, Madeline's former broke boyfriend is now her affluent husband.

"My advice to women dating out there," Madeline says, "is don't buy into the fairy tale that the man of your dreams can only be a certain type of guy who does a certain kind of work or drives a certain car. Give guys who may not fit that bill a chance; they may have great potential."

....

3 WAYS to Adjust Your Dating Attitude While You Look for Love

1. **Stop looking for a perfect package.** Ask yourself if you're perfect. You may think you're pretty darn close, but in reality perfection in people doesn't exist. The "perfect package" doesn't exist, either. You won't find a guy who has everything you want in a mate. Realize that everyone (yes, even you) has flaws.

2. **Stop looking for a high-net-worth hunk.** Sure, it would be great to find a guy with a healthy bank account when you meet him, but don't discount the guy who is working his way up the corporate ladder, starting his own business, or working two jobs to get ahead.

3. **Stop looking for a bad boy.** It may be exciting to date a guy who rides a motorcycle, has no regard for authority, and throws caution to the wind. But is that the kind of guy you want to be your husband? Nope! Remember, you want a guy who is caring, responsible, and committed. Realize that a guy who is steady, stable, and levelheaded doesn't have to equal a guy who is boring in your eyes.

PART 2

A 10-STEP GUIDE TO GETTING YOUR BROKENHEARTED BUTT IN GEAR

Break the Cycle of Dating Bad Guys

Accept That You Have a Problem

If you're like most women, at some point, you've dated jerks, gigolos, cheaters, liars, and losers, not just once, but over and over again. You know the ones—the hottie you dated who couldn't stop talking about his ex. The guy you swore you could fix by urging him to get a real job instead of making a career out of borrowing money from you. The guy you dated with mommy issues who tried to mold you into a much younger version of her. And let's not forget about the married guy who just couldn't seem to divorce the wife who had been making him miserable for years.

You're not alone. We've all (yes, me, too) dated these guys. I was an addict. But my vices weren't drugs, drinking, or prescription pill-popping—I was addicted to bad boyfriends. I never took the time to figure out why I dated the same cheaters, liars, and losers over and over again. Was there something wrong with me? I was a smart, accomplished girl and for the most part, I thought I was a pretty good girlfriend to the jerks I dated, but I just couldn't get my act together when it came to guys.

The problem was that my low self-esteem and lack of confidence caused me to ignore the glaring signs that the guys I was dating just weren't right for me. Looking back, I'm certain I ignored the signs for many reasons—because I didn't want to be alone, or because I was convinced that if I just tried a little harder, I could get the guy I was dating to change his bad behavior. Boy was I wrong!

The best thing I ever did for myself was to take a long, hard look at my relationships. It wasn't easy going back there, and I could really just kick myself for dating the cheaters, liars, and losers I dated, wasting so much of my precious time on guys who clearly weren't worth it. You probably are, too. But that's okay. Everyone makes mistakes. The thing to do now is to learn from them and make sure you don't repeat the same ones in the future.

To break *your* bad-boyfriend habit, you have to understand why you date these jerks in the first place, just like I did. Why do you keep doing the same thing over and over, with guy after guy, hoping for a different result each time? Predictably, you're always disappointed when you fall victim to a bad breakup, followed by months and months of nursing your bruised and battered heart.

Why Do We Do This to Ourselves?

There are many reasons you may be repeatedly dating guys who don't treat you right. "Bad men are exhilarating! Thrilling! Exciting! Every gal knows that," says Samantha Brett, Australia's premier female dating expert. "The trouble is that while some of us can date and leave 'em, there are others that get so caught in their treacherous web that they find themselves unable to break free—ever. So they go from one bad boy to another, craving the same excitement and thrill they had the first time—only, like a drug, it never really is the same."

According to Dr. Paul Dobransky, a board-certified MD psychiatrist in private practice and author, attraction may be to blame for your repetitive dating foibles. "Some in my field will say it's all the Freudian 'repetition compulsion'—which is true and is there: we seek the familiar, and unconsciously go back to master the past by unwittingly encouraging it to repeat," says Dobransky. "But another possibility is simply that women are passionately attracted to masculine men. You are passionately attracted and desiring of a masculine man, but what if he is also immature or otherwise lacking? Then you are attracted to an abuse situation at worst or dissatisfying relationship at best over and over again." Here are some other reasons you may be repeating your mistakes again and again.

YOU'RE FOLLOWING YOUR PARENTS' BAD EXAMPLES

Often, you're simply repeating your parents' unfortunate relationship patterns that you observed during your childhood. The dating decisions you make and relationships you choose may be rooted in the behavior of dear old mom and dad. If you spent your childhood watching your mother cry her eyes out every time your dad cheated on her, you'll probably have a natural aversion to guys who commit adultery. You grow up thinking you don't want what happened to your mother to happen to you. If you grew up watching your mom date a slew of cheaters, liars, and losers, chances are you, like many women out there, have done the same thing. Men often emulate their fathers' behavior, too. So if your last boyfriend saw his dad cheat on his mom, he may think it is acceptable male behavior to have more than one woman in his life at a time.

YOU STARTED OFF ON THE WRONG FOOT

Your first bad romantic experience also significantly shapes what kind of dater you grow up to be. Your very first heartbreak changes you forever. That's the moment the "knight in shining armor" dream you had implodes and you learn, all too painfully, that men really are just mere mortals who make mistakes and cause hurt feelings. It's a hard lesson to learn the hard way. Because you're young and vulnerable, you may be more susceptible to a dramatic breakup. And since it's your "first impression" of a breakup, it tends to stick with you and set the standard for what you assume all future breakups will be like. Though you may think a high-school boyfriend is in your distant past, you may actually be subconsciously comparing future boyfriends to him, or waiting for guys to do just what he did. Because you've never had a healthy breakup, you don't really know what one is like. It's natural for you to assume that the way you broke up with your ex is the way everyone does it. My first breakup was devastating. I was in high school and I discovered the guy I was dating was also making out with girls at a nearby high school. That's how I came to mistakenly believe that all men were inherently skirt-chasing jerks who couldn't be trusted. This view was reinforced over and over again with each bad breakup I endured.

YOU HAVE LOW SELF-ESTEEM

We talked a lot about this in the last chapter, but I'll mention it again because it's likely a factor in your bad-boy dating habit. The less you think of yourself, the less you think you deserve—so you fall for guys who are way beneath you. That's why it's so important to value yourself and give yourself credit where credit is due! When you don't, you practically invite losers to take advantage of you.

YOU'RE AFRAID TO BE ALONE

Many women keep dating guys they subconsciously know aren't right for them just because they don't want to be single. You may genuinely feel lonely without a boyfriend, or you may feel left out if most of your girlfriends are in relationships. It's perfectly okay to want a man in your life, but only if he's a great guy worthy of your love.

If you fall into this category, ask yourself what you get from a relationship that you can't get when you're alone. If it's companionship, rally your girls for a night out more often when you're single. If you feel left out or like a third wheel because your friends are in relationships, bring a guy friend or a single girlfriend along when your girls are all going out with their guys. Look for healthier alternatives to getting involved with a loser while you try to find a winner!

If You Only Knew Then What You Know Now: An Exercise

If you haven't done it already, it's time to dig into your own past and find the bad dating patterns lurking there so you can recognize and reject them. Get out your Don't Date Him, Girl list (see page 21). Next to each name, jot down five warning signs that, in retrospect, you wished you saw during your relationship with each guy.

For example, did you overlook all the girls he had on his Facebook or MySpace page, the majority of whom you had never met? When he told you he was working late, did you ignore your intuition and convince yourself he couldn't possibly be cheating on you, even when he walked in at four in the morning? When he lied to you about being worth millions, did you keep dating him anyway? Now is the time to be honest about those signs. Don't beat yourself up for not noticing them then; that's not the point here at all. You were so willing to settle back then that you couldn't see him for who he really was. You only saw what you wanted to see, and unfortunately, his flaws weren't on your list.

That's water under the bridge at this point. There's nothing you can do to change what happened. You have no control over what happened in the past. But you can control what's going to happen in the future—that's why you're doing this exercise.

ASK YOUR FAMILY AND FRIENDS

Once you've created your own Don't Date Him, Girl list, it's time to ask trusted friends and family members if they can help you out. You'll get valuable insight into your dating patterns that they've observed over the years as an outsider. Listen when they tell you about the patterns they notice you repeating in your romantic relationships. Don't be discouraged by what they say—this is not about blaming or ridiculing; it's about research.

They're just looking out for you and that's what friends are for, after all. Take notes. If your sister tells you that you always date bad boys who end up playing games with your heart, believe her. Write down everything she says. If your best friend tells you that you have a nasty habit of trying to fix the flaws of subpar guys you should never have been dating in the first place, listen to her.

LAURA'S DON'T DATE HIM, GIRL LIST

Laura, twenty-five, finally reached a breaking point and made her own Don't Date Him, Girl list. Over and over again, she spent her time with guys who wouldn't commit, refused to stay faithful, and couldn't tell the truth.

"I was friends with my husband for three years before we dated," Laura says. "A few short months after we started dating, he proposed to me. He seemed so full of charm and positivity at the time we got married. But then, a year after we got married, I began to notice little things."

That's when Laura's husband went from being close to perfect to utterly pathetic. "The night of our daughter's birth, he slept with another woman. I was in the hospital in Philadelphia and he was with his mistress in New Jersey. He spent the night with her and came to the hospital the next morning like everything was fine."

But Laura got off the bad-boyfriend roller coaster ride. She finally shined the light on her bad-boyfriend addiction. "I literally took out a piece of paper and started making a list of all the things that went wrong in my past relationships. When I was done, the mistakes were clear as day, right there on paper. I couldn't ignore them, because they were right in front of my face."

ANALYZING YOUR OWN LIST

Now it's your turn to take a good hard look at your own bad dating patterns. Look at the piece of paper containing the names of your last five boyfriends and the warning signs you wish you had recognized. See any familiar patterns? Look for his behaviors (did all three guys cheat on you?) and yours (did you always give him a second chance?). If you wrote down a lot next to each name, circle similar words or feelings to help you find common themes. You may find that you keep dating guys who need "fixing" or "mothering." Or maybe your boyfriends have all been verbally abusive. Or maybe they've all been fun-loving guys who couldn't commit long-term. Once you've found your particular pattern, ask yourself, what did you do that, in retrospect, you would never do again? Where did your instincts prove correct?

These are not easy questions to answer, I know. But this is an important step in kicking your bad-boyfriend habit. Just like Laura, once you see these habits written down on paper, you'll find them hard to ignore. Again, don't judge your actions with the twenty-twenty hindsight you have now. Instead, be proud that you're taking such a difficult step toward self-awareness. Congratulate yourself on discovering these patterns so you can avoid them in the future. You're not afraid to shed some light on your mistakes—you're bringing them out into the open so you can learn from them and move on, once and for all. It takes courage and confidence, but you can do it, girl! And now you've got your secret weapon—the list—along with you for the ride!

Kicking the Habit for Good

Now that you've narrowed down what kinds of mistakes you've been making, it'll be easier to steer clear of them in future relationships. Here are some ways to help you stop your bad-boyfriend cycle in its tracks.

TAKE RESPONSIBILITY FOR YOUR ACTIONS

Now is the time to step it up and take charge of your behavior, no matter where it came from. "Our relationship patterns are set during childhood," explains Kerry Gray, a dating expert and frequent contributor to DontDateHimGirl.com. "These patterns are hard to break, but they can be changed with only a little work on your part."

To avoid succumbing to a particular pattern from your past, take action and change your behavior. Even if your parents are part of the reason you've been dating losers thus far, you can't keep blaming them. Your parents can't change your behavior for you—you have to do that yourself.

"Once you realize you are making the same mistake over and over again, it's time to do something about it," says dating expert Alison James, author of the book *I Used to Miss Him, But My Aim Is Improving.* "You can kick a bad dating habit just like you can kick any other bad habit, but it takes willpower and work. Write down the mistakes you keep making. Put it down on paper and shine a light on it. By doing so, you'll see just how this habit has been getting in your way."

DO THE OPPOSITE

Here's another idea to try. Start doing the *opposite* of what you did when you dated losers. If you were prone to sleeping with a new guy on the first date, don't even think about it until the tenth date. If you used to loan boyfriends money, point them to the nearest bank instead.

"If you always called guys right after you met them, resolve not to call the next guy you date right away," advises Laura. "If you know you fall in love too quickly, decide to hold back the next time around, then really do it." The key is to find your bad patterns, then do an about-face and stick to it.

GET A LITTLE HELP

For reinforcement, get support from your friends and family. It's difficult to change longtime habits—ask anyone who's quit smoking—and you'll need some encouragement along the way. Start with the people you asked to help you find your bad dating patterns. They know you well and will be aware if you're slipping into old habits.

STOP THE SELF-SABOTAGE

One way to assure yourself you'll stay out of bad-boy trouble is to stop the self-sabotage that undermines your romantic relationships. You may not think that you're a serial self-sabotager, but chances are high that you are indeed unknowingly sabotaging your romantic relationships and suffering the consequences for it. We'll talk a lot more about self-sabotaging in Step 9.

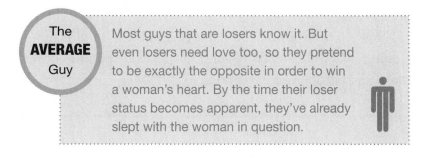

The **AVERAGE** Guy

Most guys that are losers know it. But even losers need love too, so they pretend to be exactly the opposite in order to win a woman's heart. By the time their loser status becomes apparent, they've already slept with the woman in question.

The Beginning of the Rest of Your Dating Life

After a while, dating cheaters, liars, and losers over and over again becomes exhausting. Thankfully, this time around, you're going to date differently. For starters, you're not going to let the same old undateable guys into your love life. Sure, each guy was different, but essentially they were all the same—not right for you!

You've now discovered an established dating pattern that must be broken for the sake of your future happiness. Stop ignoring the signs that the guy you're dating is clearly not right for you, and don't stay with him for silly reasons. Use your Don't Date Him, Girl list!

The point is a bastard broke your heart. Join the club! What are you going to do about it right at this very moment? Are you going to mope, sulk, and gain weight by mindlessly munching on sugary snacks, guzzling cosmopolitans, or cozying up to your couch to make yourself feel better? Sure, it's tempting, but you've got to be practical here, girl! No man is worth gaining weight over, period. And no man, under any circumstances, is worth the inevitable wrinkles you'll get from sulking over him for too long!

Now, let's make sure you're moving in the right direction— getting over your breakup—and not instead spiraling downward and becoming a bitter bitch!

Beat the Bitter Bitch Blues

Bastards Can Leave a Bad Taste in Your Mouth

It's hard *not* to become bitter after you've had your heart broken a few times. Dating cheaters, liars, and losers inevitably becomes a bitter cycle of pain, hurt feelings, and lingering bitterness. Depending on what the circumstances were surrounding the parting of ways with your exes, you may harbor resentment, anger, and even hatred. What you may not realize is that holding on to those feelings actually puts your exes in control of your romantic future. They're not even in your life anymore and you're giving them the power to decide your future. That's not cool, young lady!

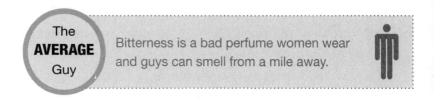

The **AVERAGE** Guy

Bitterness is a bad perfume women wear and guys can smell from a mile away.

Are You Bitter?

Brokenhearted women manifest their bitterness in different ways. Ask yourself the following questions—if you can answer "yes" to any of them, you're bitter!

- ✦ Have you hatched a dangerous revenge plot against your ex?
- ✦ Have you let that bastard harden your heart so that no man can ever love you again?
- ✦ Has this bad breakup closed you off emotionally from everyone, including your own family?
- ✦ Do you talk about your ex incessantly to anyone who will listen?

These are all signs that the effects of your breakup have gone beyond normal sadness and into bitterness. If you're bitter, you're not alone—just ask DontDateHimGirl.com members. Celeste, twenty-nine, became a bitter bitch after she learned that her husband was carrying on a torrid affair with her former yoga instructor.

"His affair destroyed my life," says Celeste. "The pain was unbearable, partly because I thought my husband would never cheat on me." Celeste discovered her former yoga instructor, whom she considered a friend, was helping her husband plan his exit from their marriage. She was betrayed not only by her ex, but by her girlfriend as well.

"They were in it together from the start," Celeste says. "It was all about how they were going to get me and my son out of the way through a quick divorce so they could be with each other. I was so angry at both of them, I couldn't see straight." When her husband moved in with the yoga instructor while they were still married, Celeste's bitterness grew.

Celeste eventually filed for divorce, but her bitterness remained. "My husband and his mistress destroyed me and my son and the family we were supposed to be," she says. "I was determined not to let either one of them forget it. Why should they just get away with hurting me and my son like this? I am definitely bitter. If we're miserable, why shouldn't they be?" So she decided to enroll in daily yoga classes taught by the woman who stole her husband.

Celeste was consumed with bitterness over her bad breakup. Yet she was only hurting herself! Sure, it was awkward for the yoga instructor, but ultimately *she* was the one going home to Celeste's husband every night, not Celeste. By showing up at her adversary's yoga class each day, Celeste continued to relive the pain of her husband's infidelity. It was like opening a deep wound every single day and then attempting to sew it back up, just so she could rip it open again the next day and repeat the same cycle of pain. For Celeste to move on and find love again, she had to let go of the bitterness that was beginning to negatively affect all areas of her life. She had to let go of what her ex and her former friend did to her.

How to Get over Bitter Bitchiness

Your ex may have done some really bad stuff to you—things you're certain you'll never forget or get over. But keeping those feelings in your present life will keep you stuck where Celeste was—in a haze of bitterness and resentment. Clear the air with these ideas.

After a bad breakup, you might be tempted to sit around analyzing what happened, looking at old pictures of the good times you and your ex had together and maybe even secretly hoping for reconciliation. But even if you were to get back together with your ex, both of you would have to make some changes in order for the relationship to work. You might be willing to do that, but he's probably not, so don't waste your time thinking about that. Instead, put your ex where he belongs—behind you! You've already broken up. Your relationship is ancient history. You can't go back and change what happened. You can't go back and make him faithful, honest, or kind, so don't waste your precious time trying. Unless your ex is paying rent to take up space in your head, kick him out of there!

Dr. Dobransky recommends that women in his practice do what men do to get over a bad breakup. "Take over a man's habits and skills at overcoming this, and feel empowered for doing so—for example, date *many* men as friends, enjoy the company of your girlfriends, go on a roadtrip, do something you've always wanted to but never had the freedom to," says Dobransky. "I use the word 'abandon' a great deal—it means TWO things: to 'be left or bereft,' or alternatively, to 'revel in the pleasure of freedom, the future, and possibility.' The choice is really up to you, and perhaps doing this with your insides is more important than what you do on the outside." So how can a single girl stop living in the past with an ex, as Dr. Dobransky recommends? Try these seven easy ways to do it quick.

....

7 WAYS to Stop Dwelling on Past Dating Disasters

1. **Face reality.** Accept that your relationship is over. Sometimes facing the aftermath of a bad breakup can be daunting. But understand you will be much better off emotionally if you can accept it and move on. It's hard, but not impossible, and since you're a smart girl, you can do it.

2. **Believe your ex this time.** If your guy dumped you and told you he didn't want to be with you anymore, believe him. Maybe he had a big problem telling you the truth in the past when you were in a relationship, but he's actually telling you the truth this time. It might be hard to accept that someone you once loved no longer loves you, but it's the truth and in order to move on you're going to have to come to grips with that. Don't sit by the phone, waiting for him to call, because he won't. Don't "just happen" to go to places you know he frequents in hopes of running into him there. He broke your heart, remember? Use your time to work on you and your future.

3. **Don't be a hater.** Whatever he did to you, don't hate him for it. It takes up too much of your precious time and energy to harbor feelings of hatred toward him. You can also become so consumed with hatred that you stop living your life for you and it becomes all about your ex. You need to get to the point where you can actually feel sorry for the bastard who broke your heart because he is really a damaged person who needs to learn how to behave properly in a romantic relationship.

4. **Create a new habit to replace your bad-boyfriend one.** After a breakup, it's important to add new activities to your routine. Exercise, learn a new language, or go back to school. You may not feel like doing anything more than sulking on your couch, but now's not the time. Right now, it's time to start adding new, fun, and exciting activities to your routine. Try something new and watch how quickly your life and your spirit change.

5. **Toss his things.** Don't save the mementos of your relationship if they cause you pain. If you still have the jewelry he gave you for your birthday, sell it and buy yourself something fabulous. If all the clothes he bought you while you dated are still hanging in your closet, donate them to a charity like Dress for Success, an organization that provides clothing for disadvantaged women to go on job interviews. If you just can't bring yourself to toss the things that remind you of him, have a girlfriend take the stuff and promise to keep it for a year. She must also promise not to provide you with access to those things for a year, though! When that year is over, you'll see, you won't even remember that you gave her those things for safekeeping.

6. **Don't befriend other bitter women.** You've heard the old phrase that misery loves company. Women who are brokenhearted want somebody to join them in their bitterness, but don't you dare join the Bitter Bitch Club. Find a group of happy, healthy women to hang out with instead and soon, you'll be just like them, bragging about your great relationship.

7. **Cut off contact.** "Have no contact for thirty days," says Kerry Gray. "Then shoot for another thirty. Pretty soon

you will be a new woman who can look at her ex and be glad it's over even if you really loved him."

The bottom line is, don't waste your precious time analyzing and remembering your relationship. Get on with your life!

FORGIVE HIS MANY SINS, BUT DON'T FORGET

Forgiving a guy who broke your heart is one of the hardest things to do when a relationship ends. When it comes to matters of the heart in particular, forgiveness between a couple or former couple can be elusive.

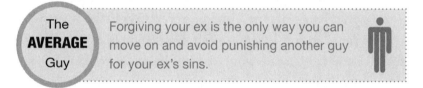

The **AVERAGE** Guy

Forgiving your ex is the only way you can move on and avoid punishing another guy for your ex's sins.

What exactly is forgiveness, anyway? In a recent article, Dr. Katherine Piderman of the Mayo Clinic wrote that forgiveness is "the decision to let go of resentments and thoughts of revenge and the act of untying yourself from thoughts and feelings that bind you to the offense committed against you." To many brokenhearted women, that's easier said than done. Forgiving a guy you love that has cheated on you, lied to you, or hurt you in some way is extremely difficult in most cases. In fact, most women in that situation would find it almost impossible!

Kim, twenty-four, knows exactly how hard it really is. "I was with a guy for over three years," Kim says. "Every night, he looked me in the eye and told me I was the love of his life. But I wasn't. He had a secret life that revolved around prostitutes and porn." Initially, Kim vowed never to forgive her ex for what he had done. But after months of harboring bitterness, she realized that the only way to heal was to forgive her ex so she could move on.

"You're not forgiving your ex for him," Kim says. "Who cares what he thinks? You're forgiving him for yourself so you don't let the bitterness eat away at your heart." Kim realized that holding on to anger, resentment, and thoughts of revenge would consume her, leaving little room in her heart to find love again.

"I was either going to sit at home dreaming up revenge plots against my ex and hating him for what he did to me," says Kim, "or, I could let go of it and open my heart up to the possibility of love again. But if I didn't forgive, instead of having an open heart, I knew my heart would be filled with hatred and anger. That's not pretty."

Forgiving an ex is hard, but not impossible, and there are very good reasons to do it.

4 REASONS to Forgive the Bastard Who Broke Your Heart

1. **You'll be happier.** You may think you'll feel like a fool, or like you've "lost," for forgiving an ex who hurt you, but in reality, you'll be a much happier person. Holding on to anger and resentment over a failed relationship is a burden that gets heavier the longer you hold it. That doesn't sound like much fun, does it?

2. **You'll be sexier.** Holding on to anger often leads an attractive woman such as yourself to create a permanent scowl on her face. Not cute! Remember that guys can

spot bitterness on a woman just as easily as they can spot a woman who is confident, secure, and resentment-free!

3. **You'll be healthier.** The anger, self-blame, and frustration you feel about your breakup can cause you to develop high levels of stress, which can open the door to many other unhealthy ailments.

4. **You'll be nicer.** Women who don't have anger in their hearts are kinder people, especially to the men they meet. Just ask Kim. "When I was walking around angry at my ex," says Kim, "I found myself angry at other people for no reason and after going to therapy for a while, I realized I wasn't angry at the people in my life who had nothing to do with my breakup. I was still angry with my ex for what he had done to me."

Need another good reason to forgive your ex? Forgiving gives *you* the power, especially when you're the one doing the forgiving. It's a powerful place for you to be emotionally. It means you are able to objectively see him for the man that he is and assess your role in the demise of the relationship.

SKIP THE REVENGE PLOT

While you're letting go of your anger, be sure to ditch any thoughts of revenge, please! We've all heard that living well is the best revenge, and guess what? It's true. Don't sit at home hatching a revenge plot against your ex. It just isn't worth it. Use that time to work on forgiving your ex, instead of trying to get him back. Nothing good is going to come of it. Your ex isn't plotting revenge against you. Guys just don't think that way.

Do you know what your ex is probably doing right now? He's at home watching football or at a restaurant wining and dining a new girl. He's having fun on the dating scene, not at home dreaming up ways to get even with you because of your breakup. So which one of you is letting this breakup hold you back? You guessed right! It's you! Besides, exacting revenge on a former flame isn't ladylike!

The **AVERAGE** Guy

Guys don't waste time thinking about revenge, because they would rather spend that time finding women to date and have sex with.

STOP TALKING ABOUT HIM ALREADY!

While talking about a breakup with your girlfriends is normal, after a while, it needs to stop. If it doesn't, you're moving into Bitter Territory. Bitterness festers when you brood about your bad breakup to anyone who will listen to you. So change your chatty ways! Don't speak to everyone you meet about how your ex cheated on, lied to, and deceived you. When you behave this way, your sad tales of romantic woe become a defining part of who you are, like a badge or name tag for everyone to see that says, "My name is _____ and I've been the victim of a bad breakup."

After a while, everyone knows your story because you've told it so many times. You've got better things to talk about, don't you? Of course you do!

Instead of talking about what he did to you, talk about how much happier you're going to be when the bastard who broke your heart is a distant memory. Talk about your plans for the future. Let everyone know what you're going to do when the pain of this bad breakup subsides. Talk about the type of guy you're hoping to attract and what you're going to do to get him. Talk about *anything* but your ex.

Every time you talk about the things he did to you, you hurl yourself right back to the past, instead of propelling yourself forward to the future. You give him all the control over your dating destiny and you put him in the driver's seat of your love life. He's the one steering the car and he's not even really in it! You're the only one who belongs in the driver's seat, young lady. What girl wants to be a passenger or back-seat driver of her own love life? What single girl wants to think about a terrible past when a bright future is just around the corner?

Vent

To end your bitching once and for all, take a cue from the nearly 1 million women who have shared their dating experiences on DontDateHimGirl.com, and post your story. It will inspire other women in the same situation to avoid a cheater, liar, or loser and find real love. But that's where it ends. You can talk about what happened to you if it's going to help another woman avoid heartache or learn from your mistakes. But then not another word about it!

Zip It with New Guys

Don't let your breakup be the only thing you talk about when you meet someone new. To guys, reliving your past relationship while they listen is a huge turnoff. And you don't want to send a potentially great guy packing because he doesn't want to carry your emotional baggage for you.

GET MENTALLY UNSTUCK

Now let's talk about how to avoid getting "stuck" in this breakup.

If you're stuck in a relationship with your ex's ghost, real men who might be good for you won't ever have a chance.

You want to be present in the here and now so you can enjoy your life, your children, your job, and the man you will one day find and love. You can't just tell yourself you're moving on, either—you can't fool yourself or a new guy. You might go out on a date and even have a relationship, but the new guy isn't in a relationship with you. He's in it with you and the ghost of your ex, too, because you won't stop talking about him. The new guy you date is the third wheel and he knows it. Most of your attention will be on your ex and not him. No guy wants to play second fiddle to your ex, and he won't waste his time waiting for you to work out your demons. Because of this, your new guy will start to resent you and before you know it, he'll do exactly what your ex did—*leave*!

DON'T WAIT FOR AN AWARD

Being a bitter bitch brings no rewards, either. Bitterness isn't pretty and you won't get a great reward for being the most bitter or harboring the most resentment. Instead of a great guy for your efforts, your reward will be crow's feet, wrinkles, Botox, and one bad breakup after another. Yuck!

DON'T GET BITTER ON YOURSELF

When you get bitter, you might start questioning everything you thought you knew about men, love, and romantic relationships. Worse, you can start questioning your own self-worth even more than before. We've already talked a lot about self-esteem, but if you've become bitter, you're just adding more fuel to the fire. Men can make you question yourself, your beauty, and whether you're really as sexy as you think you are. Don't blame men for this, though. The blame lies squarely with you on this one. Women, even really smart ones, give men the power to impact their self-esteem, confidence, and self-worth. A guy can't physically get into your head and force you to think negative thoughts about yourself. You let those thoughts in.

Most women second-guess their *bad* decisions. But when you're bitter, you might devalue your self-worth to the point that you start questioning your *good* decisions too! The problem is so prevalent that women have actually written to DontDateHimGirl.com in dire straits because they were convinced they made a huge mistake by not, say, having a threesome when their man requested one, not letting their guy have a girlfriend on the side, or not letting him have an all-boys weekend in Vegas. If your gut told you it was the right decision, it was! You should never have a threesome with a guy out of fear you will displease him and he will break up with you!

Men don't put that kind of pressure on themselves, despite the fact they are bombarded with similar advertising messages, telling them they've got to look like a strapping Adonis to be considered attractive to a woman. They just don't think like that and neither should you.

Bitter Bitches Always Get Wrinkles

Look at your breakup as an opportunity to start over. You can finally find the guy you really want, not one that you're merely willing to settle for because you can't find anyone better. But that doesn't mean there aren't many other men out there who will be enamored with how fabulous you are. Find a guy who thinks you are the best thing in his world—the woman he simply can't live without. That guy is out there, but he's not going to compete with the ghost of your ex.

So, don't walk around bitter, sporting a frown, instead of flashing your gorgeous smile. Chronic frowning because you're bitter or resentful causes wrinkles to form on your face. Erasing those horrid wrinkles costs tons of money. So not only are you brokenhearted after your breakup, but if you add bitterness to the mix, you're going to go into debt trying to erase those unsightly wrinkles you've got from frowning so much—all because some guy broke your heart. That's money that could be much better spent on stilettos, spas, and sexy dresses. You're going to need that cash to spend on stilettos and other stunning post-breakup accessories, because it's time to celebrate your breakup, then get your brokenhearted butt in gear and find a great guy!

Plan the Perfect Breakup Bash

Throw Thee a Lavish Breakup Bash

Don't feel very much like celebrating, do you? You feel like a loser in love, a girl who will never, ever find happiness with a guy, because there's either something wrong with you or all the good guys have already been taken? You're certain you're going to end up old and alone, right? Wrong! If only you could hear how pitiful you sound right now! That kind of thinking is so gloom and doom, it isn't even funny! Stop the madness, girl! Of course you'll find love again!

And the first step is to throw a Breakup Bash. Also known as the pity party, this soiree is a celebration of your newfound freedom. While a lot of dating experts say you should never pity yourself after a breakup, I disagree. You really can't avoid it. When you've had your heart ripped out by a guy you thought you were going to be with for the rest of your life, it's important to feel every icky emotion that come with the territory—hurt, anger, and yes, even pity. While breakup bashes are traditionally discouraged in the world of dating, they are actually an essential part of the healing process. Why? At your breakup bash, you aren't supposed to be moping about what happened to you at the hands of the bastard who broke your heart. You're actually supposed to be celebrating what's going to happen to you now that you've got a new lease on your love life.

Sure, your last relationship didn't work out. But so what? You've now got a brand-new chance to go out and find love again. But this time you're going to do things differently. This time you're going to learn from your past dating mistakes so you don't repeat them ever again. Now isn't that something wonderful to celebrate?

Breakup Bashes 101

Don't you wish you had this class in college? In the rest of this chapter, I'll show you how to throw yourself a perfect party. Before we start, there's one thing you need to know about breakup bashes. Your party is the *one and only* opportunity to mourn the loss of the bastard who broke your heart. It's the only time you're going to be allowed to let your grief hang out. You don't get to have two, three, or a hundred parties. You only get *one* soiree to celebrate your single status. It's a perfect way to mark the end of your breakup and the beginning of your new dating life.

Most fabulous breakup bashes are intimate affairs held at home, but you can throw yours anywhere that you're com-fortable. To get started, set a date for your party. Try the Seven-Day Breakup Bash Rule. Take a look at the date today and schedule your soiree seven days from today's date. Seven days is enough time to plan just about anything, including a fabulous breakup bash! And if your bash falls on a weekday, don't worry—any day of the week is a good one for a breakup bash.

Create a Party Theme

Whether you want an evening shindig or an afternoon fete, you can get creative with your theme and you don't have to put in a lot of effort. If you're stuck for an idea, think of what your last relationship was missing, then fill that hole with your party! Here are some ideas:

- When you were with your ex, did you always joke to your friends that he was lousy in bed? Now that you don't have to deal with his pathetic puny penis anymore, celebrate by throwing a lingerie party for just you and your best girlfriends. Sport your best leather or lace lingerie for the occasion.
- Did your ex hate Caribbean music, but you absolutely love it? For your pity party, plan an island-themed fete complete with rum punch and reggae music!
- If you had the bad habit of making up for your ex's personal budget deficit by giving him money, throw your bash at a spa and spend some money on yourself for once.
- Was your ex so boring in the bedroom that he didn't want to role-play with you? Then throw a lavish costume party and play dress-up. You could be anything you want—a sexy siren, a naughty schoolgirl, or a sultry nurse.

Create the Guest List

Are you going to celebrate by yourself or are you going to invite guests?

"When I threw myself a breakup bash," says Annette, twenty-eight, "I invited all of my girlfriends, a few of my coworkers, and even my neighbor. I wasn't going to party by myself!" You may be like Annette and have a list of people a mile along you want to celebrate your breakup with.

But if you want, you can throw a breakup bash for one. You can spend the day alone at the spa with just your masseuse, or you can pass the time having a romantic comedy movie marathon. Either option is okay—just choose what works best for your personality.

Pick a Party Spot

Choose a location according to your theme. If you're doing a spa day, of course your location is the spa. If you're hosting the party at your home or apartment, consider decorating one or two rooms where the majority of the party will be held. If you're heading to your favorite nightspot, call ahead and see if you can reserve a table or sitting area so you have some space to yourselves.

Carol, thirty-eight, held a breakup bash at her house when her husband of ten years broke up with her for a woman he met online. "I knew our marriage was over," Carol says, "but I didn't want to turn into one of those women who sat around bitter, unable to move on with her life. So I threw a pity party to celebrate my newfound freedom."

Carol always wanted her ex to take her to a tropical island. "He kept telling me throughout our entire marriage that he was going to take me to Jamaica one day," she says, "but he never did." Carol later found out that her ex did go to Jamaica a few weeks after their breakup with the girl he met online. "I couldn't believe he had done that," Carol says. "Looking back, I never really realized what a jerk he was."

So when Carol threw her breakup bash, she brought Jamaica to her living room. "I used a Caribbean theme complete with island music and margaritas," says Carol. "I invited a few of my girlfriends and we had a great time! The party really lifted my spirits and gave me the strength to move on. It inspired me to continue the journey to healing my broken heart."

Send Out Cute Invites

If you decide you're inviting other people, get invitations out sooner rather than later (especially if you're following the Seven-Day Rule). To ease the burden on the environment, skip the paper ones and send cute invites by e-mail! Your best bet is to create invitations according to the theme you selected. Check out *www.evite.com*, *www.MyPunchBowl.com*, or *www.Pingg.com* for a plethora of options.

> **The AVERAGE Guy**
>
> Like girls, guys have breakup bashes, too, but they may involve liquor and strippers, not a pretty party dress.

Pick a Pretty Party Dress

You've set the date, picked a theme, and secured a location for your party. But what are you going to wear? A single girl like you can't show up at her breakup bash dressed inappropriately. You need a fabulous, form-fitting sexy little number that will make you feel like the princess that you are!

Your breakup bash requires you to purchase a pretty dress for the occasion. Check out your favorite boutiques, consignment shops, and department stores for something slinky. Even if you're just going to the spa for a day, get glamorous so that when you enter, everyone's heads will turn. It's more symbolic than anything, but getting dressed up can be a great self-esteem booster.

Grab the sexiest dress you find on the sale rack and own it. The perfect breakup bash dress is one you would never normally wear. Remember your alter ego! Shake things up a little and wear something no one would ever expect you to own. Be bold and brave. Select a dress that celebrates the strong, confident woman you're going to become after this breakup.

Choose bright colors instead of basic black. It's not a funeral, despite the fact that you may feel like crying. It's a party, so ditch the dark colors and opt for something vibrant. Go for a bold color like a brilliant yellow or scarlet red.

This is a party dedicated to your fabulous dating future, so invest in a dress that is going to make you feel glamorous and put you in the mood to have fun. Wipe away the tears you've been shedding, slip into your perfect dress, and let's party!

Purge the Pain

Your breakup bash is going to be great! It's a celebration of your future. You know you're going to have fun, but the pain your ex caused you is still there. Your heart is hurting. That's to be expected when it's broken. It's going to feel like that for some time—not long, but you've still got a little ways to go before your heart is completely healed. Until then, try these three easy ways to purge the pain of this breakup from your system fast!

3 WAYS to Purge Your Pain Fast

1. **Don't avoid your pain.** It's there and you're going to feel it for a while. Don't do anything to try to cover it up or pretend it doesn't exist, because it does. It hurts, but you're going to have to acknowledge it in order to get over it. Also, don't do things like drink or party every weekend to make yourself feel better. When the party ends and you sober up, the pain will still be there for you to deal with. Isn't it better to feel it, purge it from your system, and move on?

2. **Concentrate on you.** Now is the time to be selfish about yourself! In your past dating relationships, you probably gave too much of yourself to the guys you dated. You put your needs, wants, and feelings aside in favor of what they wanted or needed. Because you're so used to doing that, after a while, you can forget that you even exist at all. What

you want goes by the wayside. Now that you're single and free, forget about everyone else! Who cares what your ex thinks? Who cares what your parents think? No one else's opinion matters now. Clear the clutter from your life and focus on the things you want and need.

3. **Make an action plan.** You're the only one who really knows what you want out of life. You know what's going to make you happy. You know what you want to accomplish in life. So what are you waiting for, girl? Write it down and do what you need to do so you can make it happen. You'll be surprised how quickly you'll forget about this breakup when you've got a list of things to do that only involve you!

Okay, you're starting to get the idea here. You're starting to understand how important it is to feel the emotions you're feeling right now and then purge them from your system so you can find love again. Here are some more ideas on how to get over the pain fast.

MARK YOUR CALENDAR

The last thing you want is to feel the pain of this breakup forever. Well, you don't have to! You're the one who decides how long you hurt. You can prolong the agony and let weeks, months, and years pass before you finally get over the guy who hurt you. Or you can make it quick by setting a deadline for your sulking. Your breakup bash is the perfect day to call it quits on the sulking. Whether it's a month or two after your breakup, make your breakup bash the very last day that you're going to sulk over your ex. Make it the very last day that you feel bad about yourself over this breakup. Make it the last day you get down on yourself because you lost a guy you thought was the one for you.

Once you set the date for your bash, make a vow to yourself that after that day, you will sulk no more. You will move on with your love life and change it for the better.

CRY

It's okay to shed tears. It's even okay to feel like crap and sulk for a while. It's definitely not okay to do either one of those things forever, however. Purging the pain from your system means empowering yourself to stick to your deadline and doing everything you can to avoid thinking about, dwelling on, or trying to figure what led to this breakup.

SET A PENALTY

The longer you mope, the more time it's going to take you to heal that broken heart of yours. For good measure, establish a penalty for sulking about your ex after the deadline you set for yourself. You'll need some willpower, but making the commitment to move on is essential. If you need to enlist the help of your girlfriends to enforce it, do so. That's what Sandra, twenty-three, did.

"My girlfriends and I picked a date about three months after my ex broke my heart," says Sandra. "I told my friends that if they saw me moping around, sad about the fact that I was single or sulking because I heard something about my ex and his new girlfriend, I would pay them $1."

That really worked for Sandra. "Once I had paid them about $50 or so, I realized that sulking was starting to have a really negative effect on my bank account," Sandra says. "Seeing how much money I was 'spending' to sulk really put things in perspective for me and I stopped." Sandra could have turned her breakup into a long, expensive, dramatic soap opera, but she didn't and neither are you.

Toast to Your Future Dating Success

While all of your friends are gathered at your breakup bash, take an opportunity to toast to your dating future. Give out cute paper as a party favor so that each of your girlfriends can make their own Don't Date Him, Girl list. Thank all your friends for their support during this horrible breakup and remind them how special they are to you. You can also do something dramatic, such as taking his picture out of a frame and ripping it up for all to see, a symbol of the fact that you've cleaned house in your love life. Do what makes you feel good. It's your bash, after all!

Breakup Bash Success Stories

Alexandra, twenty-six, was a poster child for pity after breaking up with a guy she dated for over five years. She was all set to marry him—she even had her dress picked out. "It was devastating," says Alexandra. "I planned every waking moment around this guy, moved to a different city to be with him, and starting planning a wedding after he proposed. I found out he was having sex with one of his coworkers," Alexandra says. "He said he was doing it because he knew that after he married me, he was never going to be able to have sex with another woman again."

The breakup wasn't Alexandra's fault. In fact, she wasn't to blame at all. Her ex just had a warped sense of what it means to be in a committed relationship. Although she didn't bear any blame, the horrible feelings of pity stuck. "I didn't know what to do," Alexandra says. "I knew our relationship was over, but I just didn't know how I was ever going to get over it, especially since I was just weeks away from sending out my wedding invitations."

Instead, after the breakup she sent out party invites! "One of my girlfriends suggested we have a party to celebrate my breakup," says Alexandra.

Think a breakup bash isn't the thing for you? Guess again, girl! Even famous Hollywood actresses throw them when a bad breakup strikes.

In 2005, Jennifer Aniston admitted that even she—rich, pretty, and talented—threw herself one when she broke up with Brad Pitt. "Do I have my days when I've thrown a little pity party for myself? Absolutely," Aniston told *Vogue* magazine.

What to Do When the Clock Strikes Midnight

Hopefully, your breakup bash was a blast! You've had a chance to exorcise the demons of your disastrous former relationship from your life. You're no longer the sad woman who turned to this book because you needed to know how to handle your awful breakup. That's not you! Instead, each day you're getting stronger emotionally and more ready to conquer the dating world once again. See how great throwing yourself a party can be?

DON'T CONTINUE PARTYING

Because it was such a success, you might now be tempted to party your way through this entire breakup. If you're thinking like this, stop right there! Don't do it, girl! Sure, partying is fun, but if you're doing it to forget about the pain of your recent bad breakup, it's not worth it. You're partying for all the wrong reasons and that can lead to chaos. You're not going out to have fun with your friends and blow off some steam. You're going out to drown your sorrows in booze, random men, and maybe meaningless sex. That is not attractive, girl! Remember that partying can become addictive and you're not an addict. At one time, you were addicted to bad boyfriends and had created quite a nasty little habit for yourself, but you'll never do that again, will you?

DON'T LOOK OVER YOUR SHOULDER FOR YOUR EX

If you're partying all the time because you hope your ex will walk in, see how much fun you're having, and realize what a jerk he was for breaking up with you—stop! It won't happen! Your ex doesn't have time for that and he doesn't care what you're doing or who you're sleeping with. He's already moved on (maybe with another woman) and is quite happy living his own life without you in it. His life doesn't revolve around you anymore. But don't worry, you'll soon be quite happily living your own life without *him*!

DON'T OVERINDULGE IN ALCOHOL

Another terrific reason to curb your breakup bash yearnings is that the cosmos you are sure to drink when you're at the bar have lasting, nasty effects on your pretty skin. Alcohol use promotes premature wrinkling. Dr. Nicholas Perricone, author of *The Wrinkle Cure*, warns women against excessive alcohol consumption because of the horrible affects it has on aging. "Alcohol in excess results in a rapid and sustained increase in blood sugar, which we now know is pro-inflammatory and causes the glycation reaction," Perricone wrote in an article on WebMD.com. "In addition, alcohol is metabolized by the liver to toxic chemicals called aldehydes and ketones, which are toxic to cells and are pro-inflammatory. Alcohol also dehydrates us, and when we are dehydrated, our skin looks terrible and we are also in a pro-inflammatory state that accelerates the aging process." If you use it for years to curb the pain of a breakup, you're going to end up looking years older than you really are. What woman is going to do that all over some heartbreaking bastard? Not many! Don't you be one of them!

....

3 SIGNS You're Partying *Too* Much

1. **You're gaining weight.** If you're after breakup party binge is causing you to gain weight, you've gone too far. Stop the partying and start getting your figure back, pronto!
2. **You're alienating your friends.** If you haven't seen your friends for a while because you're out partying every night in honor of this breakup, you're going overboard. It's time to put a cork in it!

3. **You're getting sloppy at work.** If you're partying until 5 A.M. day after day because of this breakup and going in to work hung-over, your performance on the job is going to suffer.

Get Off the Couch

Don't Cozy Up to Your Couch

Getting over your last breakup and getting the courage to start dating again are two different challenges. Even if you've finally gotten over your ex in Steps 1 through 3, you still have to get yourself psyched up to meet some new guys. You probably think you're not ready yet. You can't possibly get back on the dating scene sporting your sexiest black dress this soon, can you? Don't worry, you can and you will.

Think about how far you've come already. In the time it's taken you to read just about half of this book, you've made major progress. You've identified your bad-boyfriend habit, you figured out how to kick it, you've reclaimed your self-esteem, and you've celebrated your breakup. What an accomplishment, young lady! You should be very proud of yourself. You've taken a huge step on the journey to healing your broken heart and soon it's going to pay off handsomely.

Let's start with some low-stress ways to get out and about again. After all, you can't live on your couch like it's the new hotspot in town, because you know it's not. You also know that there are no guys on your couch qualified to date you, so why would you spend so much time there? Check out these five super-easy ways to get your brokenhearted butt in gear—they are *so* easy you have no excuse why you can't do them!

....

5 SIMPLE Ways to Get Off the Couch

1. **Head out.** Make it your business to get up and get out of the house at least twice every day. Whether you run out for coffee, hit the mall, or just hang out at your local bookstore, get your brokenhearted butt moving by literally moving it!

2. **Dream a little dream.** Head out to a park, find a spot to lounge, and just daydream about your life, what you want out of it, and how you're going to get it. This is a great exercise that will get you off the couch and out into the fresh air. It's just what you need to revive your spirit. Who knows? You might just meet a great guy while you're out, too!

3. **Help a friend in need.** Sometimes the best distraction from your own heartache is the heartache or problems of another. If you've got a friend who needs help, advice, or just companionship, get your butt in gear and help out! If all your friends are in great shape, volunteer at a local charity instead.

4. **See a movie, all by yourself.** Check out an afternoon matinee at your favorite theater all by yourself. Maybe there's a cute guy there alone too. . . .

5. **Buy lingerie.** Making a run to the nearest Victoria's Secret is going to get you out of the house and lift your spirits at

the same time. You may not think so, but buying yourself something sexy puts you in the frame of mind to think positively about yourself. Just picture wearing something slinky for the great guy you're ultimately going to find one day.

You Just Have to Jump In

If those five quick ways weren't enough to motivate you to get back on the dating scene, that's okay. This may take some time. After all, your couch is probably really comfy, and there's a nice TV in front of it where you can watch soap operas, sappy romantic comedies, and raucous reality shows about dating and relationships. The kitchen's probably really close, too, so you can drown your sorrows in Doritos while you watch. Admittedly, your couch is a great place to nurse a broken heart. But don't be tempted.

"While it's okay to take a few days to mourn the loss of your relationship after a breakup, you're not going to think or drink your way out of it," says Alison James. "You have to get off the couch and take action to heal your broken heart." Remember: While you're eyeing the cozy comfort of your couch, your ex is out living his life. He's not holed up at home moping on his couch, aimlessly angling the remote in front of the TV and hoping he'll find love again. You shouldn't be, either!

Now is not the time to cut yourself off from the rest of the world while you languish on your couch. You just need a little more encouragement. Yes, the thought of meeting new guys is nerve-wracking. After a bad breakup, the last thing you want to think about is finding another guy who could potentially break your heart, too. But that's not the right way to look at it. It's either you date again or you get an early start on your new life as a lonely, bitter spinster. You're either going to get your broken-hearted butt in gear or not. It's really just that simple. That's the choice Martine faced after breaking up with her fiancé last year.

Martine wallowed in self-pity, felt like it was all her fault, and ultimately vowed never to date again. "I decided that this was the last time I was going to give my heart to a man," Martine says. "I was convinced that any guy I got involved with would break my heart."

Three months after her breakup, Martine reluctantly went out on a blind date set up by friends. "I was so scared," she says. "I hadn't been out on a date in forever." But Martine slowly got her confidence back. "After a few successful dates, my self-esteem was at an all-time high," Martine says. "I felt more confident with each date and eventually, I found my Mr. Perfect."

Don't worry. After you've got a couple of dates under your belt, you'll be just like Martine—strong, confident, and sexy. Before you know it, you'll be surrounded by dashing gentleman, hanging with hot hunks, and gazing at gorgeous guys, and you know what? You won't even think twice about it! Being confident is naturally going to become a part of who you are, like your eye color or your own name.

Remember, Dating Is Exciting!

When you think about the prospect of dating again, don't look at it as a chore that you're reluctant to do because you're inevitably going to get hurt. Look at dating as an adventure—a journey that will end in you being healthy, happy, and in love with a guy who deserves you. Embrace your new adventure and use it as a means to find true love. Remember that exciting, butterflies-in-the-stomach feeling that comes with meeting a new guy? Find that feeling again!

After she broke up with her boyfriend, Anita, twenty-five, was the poster girl for misery. She was still bitter about the way things ended between her and her ex. Back then, Anita couldn't even think about getting her brokenhearted butt in gear to find a new guy. "All I did was go to work, come home, and sit on my couch, crying, reliving the relationship, and wracking my brain to figure out what I had done wrong," Anita says. "I did this over and over again, every day for months."

That's when Anita's girlfriends took action. "My best friend just came over one morning and told me that it had been months and I was going on a date with a guy friend of hers," says Anita. "I didn't want to do it, but I did."

Turns out, it was exactly what Anita needed to get herself off the couch. "I saw light at the end of the tunnel," she says. "I figured that if I could go out on a couple of good dates, then why not a few more? Even when I didn't really feel like it, I got off the couch, got dressed up, and went out with the mindset that I was going to have fun because I deserved it!" Anita found that exciting feeling that gets you off the couch and out on dates.

"Don't fear not finding the right guy or being alone," advises Alison James. "Often we stay in relationships that aren't right for us just so we can have a warm body around. It's better to be single than to be in a bad relationship. So as you're getting ready to get back out on the dating scene, don't settle. The time you waste on the wrong guy is better spent looking for the right one."

Do It for Someone Else

If you're having trouble moving on for your own sake, consider others in your life. Are your friends and family calling you AWOL? Are your kids tired of seeing you unhappy and mopey? Have you missed Happy Hour with your coworkers lately? Get out for their sake! Those people miss the happy, funny, social person they know and love. If you meet a guy, check your Don't Date Him, Girl list first, so you'll know instantly how to recognize a loser. So take a deep breath and get your brokenhearted butt out there, even if you're doing it for someone else at the moment.

Christine, thirty-one, did it for her kids. She thought her couch was another appendage growing out of her body when she divorced her husband of five years after she caught him cheating on her. She let her sadness and self-pity get the best of her. After basically living on her couch for two months, Christine finally got her brokenhearted butt in gear. "I knew I had to get over this divorce not only for myself but for my kids. They needed me."

Christine ventured out into the dating scene and eventually found the man of her dreams. "That was not easy," she admits. "But I wasn't going to let this divorce get the best of me and I don't think any woman out there should let a breakup get the best of her, either. Get up and get moving. There's a great guy waiting for you out there!"

If Christine can do it, why can't you? Sure, it's easy to live the rest of your days bonding with your couch, but wouldn't it be better to bond with a hot guy instead? Of course. But, you're not going to meet him on your couch, girl!

Bring Your Sexy Back

Think you don't have sexy in you? You couldn't be more wrong! You're gorgeous and you know it, but under all those layers of pity and self-doubt, it's hard to find the sexy girl you used to be before this breakup. But you can bring your sexy back just like Emily, thirty-three, did.

"When I broke up with my boyfriend two years ago, I felt hideous," Emily says. "You would have sworn that I'd gained two hundred pounds and grew a third eye."

The AVERAGE Guy

Guys are initially attracted to how you look, and then they decide if they like your personality enough to date you.

Although that wasn't true, Emily was convinced that she was the ugliest thing on Earth. She was certain other guys saw her that way, too. For a while, lovelorn Emily snuggled up to her couch like it was her ex. She refused to leave her apartment. "I was one of the most pitiful women you have ever seen after my breakup," says Emily. "Bringing my sexy back was not even a thought in my mind at that time."

Because Emily's confidence was shattered, she no longer thought she was attractive to the opposite sex. "I actually believed that if my own ex-boyfriend didn't want to be with me, no other guy would," Emily says. "How dumb was that?"

That was really dumb, because in reality it doesn't matter that your ex broke your heart. What's done is done and it's not going to change because you decide you're going to wear your couch out by parking yourself permanently on it. What matters now is that you heal that broken heart of yours. It's not a great position to be in, but the good news is that it isn't going to last forever. The pain will stop and you will move on and believe it or not, you will find love again.

"There came a point when I knew I couldn't live with a broken heart anymore," Emily says. "I had to quit moping and move on with my life or else I was never going to find someone." Emily knew that if she didn't get her brokenhearted butt in gear, she was destined for a life of unhappiness and misery (not to mention the weight gain she would have had to endure from cozying up to her couch). She convinced herself that she was indeed sexy enough to hit the dating scene again.

"I knew I had to bring my sexy back," says Emily. "I just didn't know how to do it." Emily learned quickly that being sexy is more a state of mind than the dress or high heels you wear. "I knew that feeling sexy wasn't about the dress or shoes; it was about me and the way I felt about myself."

What can you do to bring your sexy back after a breakup? "Start by changing just one thing about yourself," Emily suggests. "That's what I did. So if you were a brunette when you were with your ex, go red this time around. If you never dared to wear a mini-skirt and sky-high heels when you were with him, try it now and see how many confidence-boosting looks you get when you're out."

Need more ideas? In a recent online poll, DontDateHimGirl .com users suggested trying these creative ways to make sexy one of the most used words in your personal vocabulary!

....

3 WAYS to Bring Your Sexy Back

1. **Get naked.** Check yourself out in the mirror. How do you look? If you're not happy with what you see, do something about it. Be honest with yourself. If you believe that you need to lose weight, then do it. "You don't have to look like a model to have a great dating life," says the Average Guy. "The things that stand out more about a woman are how confident she is and how much she smiles. That's what men find attractive." Are you smiling enough?

2. **Go to the mall, but not to shop.** Go to the makeup counter of Nordstrom's, Macy's, or any other major department store and tell the person at the counter that you've broken up with a guy. She'll know exactly what to do. "I did this once after breaking up with my boyfriend after a year," says Amy, thirty-four. "I highly recommend this as one of the first things a woman needs to do when she gets ready to get back into the dating scene."

3. **Get physical.** It's doesn't matter if you need to lose weight or not. Exercise should be a part of every woman's beauty regimen. It's one of the fastest ways to bring your sexy back. Exercising at least three times a week will transform your body and give you a great boost of confidence at the same time. "After I ditched my boyfriend, I got

really focused and lost twenty-five pounds," says Peyton, a twenty-seven-year-old teacher. "Going through that breakup with him was the best thing I ever did for myself and for my body."

Try doing these three things for just one month. You will get tighter from the exercise, sexier from the makeover, score tons of free makeup samples, and be happier from the control you now have over your own life. See, dealing with your breakup isn't so bad, is it? You've just got to be a bit creative!

What Would Your Alter Ego Do?

Inside every woman lies the soul of a confident, sultry, stiletto-clad diva. She's just buried under a mountain of anger, resentment, and a really bad breakup right now. Your mission, should you chose to accept it, is to come out from under the wreckage of your past relationship and find your inner diva again. The first place you're going to look for her is in your own closet. . . .

1. FIND SOME CLASSY CLOTHES

Why start in the closet? Because that's where you're going to find the essential attire that every diva needs. Lately, you've probably been cocooning yourself in layers of baggy sweatpants and worn T-shirts. But that's not sexy. You don't get any extra diva points for spending all day looking like you just jumped off the treadmill. But you *can* earn points by ditching your frumpy attire in favor of the sexy outfits you used to wear before your ex broke your heart.

"Men are not looking at your clothes as much as you would think," says the Average Guy. "We just want to know that the woman we're attracted to doesn't have to wear layers of makeup to look presentable each day." Men don't know Gucci from Gap. They just want to know whether or not you look good, so spend less time on the pricey designer brand-name clothing and more time on your hair, nails, and skin. You can even wear a T-shirt and jeans, as long as your hair and makeup look presentable.

> **The AVERAGE Guy**
>
> Workout wear isn't sexy, so stop walking around all day wearing it.

To bring your diva back, you must know the difference between what types of clothing and behavior are slutty and which are sexy. Dressing sexy will go a long way in keeping your inner diva alive and helping you find love again.

Granted, showing too much skin is going to attract guys' attention when you walk into a room. But they're not going to be the guys you want to spend time with. Good guys will assume you are a certain kind of woman (not the good kind) if you wear low-cut blouses or barely there micro miniskirts. You don't want to be mistaken for a hooker, so please don't dress like one. If you do, you will just attract men who want to sleep with you because they assume you were advertising your services through your outfit.

"Less is definitely more when it comes to women's clothing," says the Average Guy. "You don't have to put your precious assets on display for the world to see in order to attract a decent guy."

Think about what pops into your mind when *you* meet a guy. The first thing you're going to notice is the way he looks and how he's dressed. Now imagine that new guy wearing sweatpants and a T-shirt approaching you. He gives off the pizza and beer stench with a laziness vibe thrown in just to seal the deal. Unless he apologizes for his appearance and gives you an explanation for it, he's going to come across like a slob in sweatpants. Yuck!

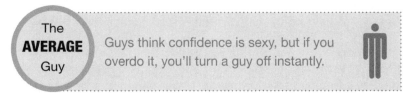

The **AVERAGE** Guy

Guys think confidence is sexy, but if you overdo it, you'll turn a guy off instantly.

Now, if, instead of wearing raggedy sweats, that same guy wore a nice pair of jeans and a white T-shirt when you met him, you might think he was actually quite sexy. In dating, it's all in the presentation, so make sure you present yourself well when you're in public. You never know when you'll find yourself crossing paths with the man of your dreams. . . .

2. EVALUATE YOUR BEAUTY REGIMEN: WHAT WOULD A DIVA DO?

You can also find your inner diva by altering your daily beauty routine. When in doubt, ask yourself—what would a diva do? A diva would make sure her hands and feet were well manicured at all times. If you've been so anxiety-ridden over your breakup that you chewed off all your fingernails like a rabid dog (very unattractive, BTW), go get them fixed. Make it your mission to look polished when you go out. That's what a diva would do. You don't have to be runway ready every time you leave your house, but you need to put a little effort into looking nice.

3. CHECK OUT YOUR HAIRSTYLE

Divas also take care of their hair. Don't go out with mangled bangs and sordid split ends. No man would be attracted to a spectacle like that. From the time you get up in the morning, have the mindset that at any moment, you could meet the man of your dreams, so you've got to be prepared. Stringy hair and a pitiful ponytail won't get guys flocking to be near you. In fact, you'll just turn them off and they'll go running in the opposite direction—all because you didn't take the time to display your inner diva. If you're really in a rush, pull your hair back and put on a little makeup when you're going to run errands.

Meet Mr. Right Now

Rebound Like a Rock Star

You've no doubt heard of rebound guys—the men you date casually when you're getting over a serious breakup. Some women don't like them. They think they're a waste of time and energy. They don't think rebound guys are essential accessories that every woman must have to heal her heart after a bad breakup. With good reason. Rebound relationships have the potential to get complicated if you don't know what you're doing. It may start out as "no strings attached" between you and your rebound guy, but the relationship can end in disaster when one, or both of you, develops real feelings for the other. In most cases, those feelings aren't mutual and one person in the equation ends up getting hurt. But that won't happen to you. After reading this chapter, you'll know that a rebound relationship is essential after a breakup and you'll know exactly how to conduct one to your benefit.

Why Is a Rebound Relationship a Good Idea?

Think of a rebound relationship as what it really is—an opportunity to practice and sharpen your rusty dating techniques. It's also a great opportunity to test out your Don't Date Him, Girl list to see if you recognize any of the signs in your rebound guy that you should have recognized about your exes. You were probably with your last ex for quite a while, so now, you're a bit out of practice. A rebound guy, although not a good candidate for the role of your ultimate Mr. Right, is just perfect for the role of Mr. Right Now. Think of your rebound guy as your love tutor of sorts. Once you've learned everything from him you can, you won't need his dating lessons anymore. Yes, it was fun and you're going to wish you could stick around and have more time with your rebound guy, but sadly, it's not meant to be. Here's a list of the five benefits of a rebound relationship.

....

5 BENEFITS of a Rebound Relationship

1. **You build self-confidence by getting out of the house and back onto the dating scene in a casual way.** Your rebound guy isn't going to be your husband, so date him to sharpen your skills and get your feet wet on the dating scene again.

2. **You can meet a variety of guys (all of whom are unlike any of the losers of your past!) and figure out which personality fits you best.** Your rebound guys can be from all walks of life, except that of your loser ex. By dating different guys without a major commitment, you get to see which kinds of men might fit you best in a relationship.

3. **You can dip your toes in the relationship pool again without putting your heart "out there" yet.**
4. **You can use your rebound guy as a dating sounding board.** You can talk to him about relationships and get insight into the way guys really think.
5. **You can use your rebound guy to gain perspective.** Dating a rebound will give you a clear picture of the types of guys you want to be with and the ones you don't want to spend a single second with.

The Secret to a Successful Rebound Relationship

Rebound relationships don't have to end in disaster if you do it the right way. The lovely Jennifer Aniston did it right when she rebounded with fellow actor Vince Vaughn after her split with hunky ex-hubby Brad Pitt. And although their rebound relationship eventually fizzled, they are still great friends today. Aniston even has an endearing nickname for Vaughn: She calls him her "defibrillator," because he helped her nurse the heart that Brad Pitt broke.

When you find a potential rebound guy, tell him upfront that you've just had your heart broken by your ex and you're only looking for a guy to casually hang out with. That's the key to the whole arrangement—letting the guy know where you stand from the start. You don't want a boyfriend and you don't want a future husband. In fact, what you really want is a few weeks of fun with a guy to take your mind off your breakup. You want to enjoy yourself without the promise of any further commitment whatsoever. Your chosen rebound guy will probably salivate at that thought, but that's beside the point! This is about you getting over this breakup, and one of the best ways to do that is with a hunky rebound guy in tow.

"I was a girl's rebound guy once," says Antonio, thirty-one. "I didn't mind because the woman I dated told me what happened to her and I knew when I heard the story that she wasn't going to be ready for a real relationship anytime soon. We had lots of fun and I still hang out with her as friends to this day." When you set the parameters of your rebound relationship upfront, everyone involved is on the same page and the relationship serves its purpose.

"My rebound guy was wonderful," says Cassandra, thirty-three. "After my divorce, I was happy to have a romantic distraction for a while. I was scared about getting out there and dating again, but through my rebound, I learned what I really wanted in a man. In the end, we both moved on and we're actually still friends."

When to Rebound

You can start rebounding shortly after a breakup, but ultimately, the timeline is up to you. There's no set time for when you should do it. You should probably start thinking about it a few weeks after the dust has settled on your disastrous breakup. But don't do it too soon. Wait until you've created your alter ego and had your breakup bash first! The right time is when the wounds of your breakup are still somewhat fresh so you can't get really into a new guy because your heart isn't fully healed yet. When you get a rebound guy, your relationship with him is going to be the casual, going out for coffee and maybe a little meaningless (but safe) sex kind of affair, rather than an engagement, wedding dress, spend the rest of our lives together kind of union. Still, you need to be in the right mindset.

Don't Get Too Involved

Even if you tell yourself that you won't really fall for your rebound guy, sometimes it's difficult not to. You might immediately compare him to your ex and realize he's so much better, so he must be Mr. Right! But hold back, girl. Remember that your heart is still healing and you're probably not seeing straight. Keep it casual and remember your goal: retrain yourself for serious dating.

"When I met my rebound guy," says Sophie, twenty-five, "he was simply amazing. He was such a gentleman and so kind to me that I started having feelings for him, but I was such a mess from my breakup that I didn't realize this guy wasn't the one for me in the long run. Although he was a great person, we both knew it wasn't going to last. But because I wanted to feel the love of another guy so badly to avoid the hurt I was carrying around from my ex, I was getting dangerously close to falling in love with my rebound guy and having another bad breakup on my hands."

After a few weeks, Sophie was able to end her rebound relationship and move on. "At first it wasn't easy," Sophie admits. "I missed my rebound guy and wanted to call him or make plans to see him." But Sophie never did. "We both said from the very beginning that we didn't want a long-term relationship," says Sophie. See how the honest upfront communication helps? "I was a mess after my breakup and in no condition to even think about seriously dating a guy. I think my rebound knew that, too."

Here's how you can keep your rebound guy in his proper place.

....

3 WAYS to Avoid Falling for Your Rebound Guy

1. **Don't go into too much detail.** One of the sure-fire ways to develop feelings for your rebound guy is to get involved in the details of his life. You can get together to go out, have dinner, and have a nice time, but don't get too involved in his life and don't let him get too involved in yours.

2. **Don't use him as a shoulder to cry on.** After a bad breakup, you're looking for people to commiserate with. Don't make your rebound guy one of them. Using your rebound guy as an emotional crutch and talking to him about the sordid details of what happened with your ex all the time could lead you to develop romantic feelings for him.

3. **Limit the amount of time you spend with your rebound guy.** Going on an occasional date with your rebound guy is fine, but trying to make him your boyfriend by seeing him all the time isn't going to work. Limit your dates to a few times a month and leave it at that. Remember, you're using your rebound guy to practice your dating skills, not trying to turn him into your husband.

Where to Meet a Rebound Guy

It's a fact. Dating experts everywhere agree that you won't find a steady boyfriend in a bar. "It's like trying to find a needle in a haystack," warns dating expert Alison James. "It's just not possible, so don't waste your time in a bar in hopes of finding the perfect guy." What you *will* find in a bar, however, is a rebound guy. So hit up some bars to grab a cocktail or snag a rebound guy, then have fun, drink responsibly, bone up on your dating skills, and move on. Here are some other great places to meet a rebound guy:

- **Go to a sporting event.** Rebound guys abound at basketball courts, soccer practices, and football games.
- **Hit the gym, but not to work out.** This is a great place to meet a guy who you won't be pumping iron with long-term. If you see a potential rebound candidate sweating it out in the free-weight area, go over and ask him if he's using a certain set of weights. From there, strike up a conversation and see where it takes you!
- **Grab a cup of coffee.** Check out your favorite coffee house and look for the guys sitting alone sipping their Joe. There's bound to be a good rebound candidate in the bunch.

Janine, twenty-nine, found her rebound guy in a bar after ending a serious relationship with her ex. "I met a guy in a bar once," says Janine. "We had a great time together, but after three months of dating him, I found out he was also dating three other girls who frequented the bar. After that, I decided to stop going there." With her rebound guy, Janine practiced her flirting, kissing, and conversation, but she knew he wasn't going to be around forever. "It was clear he wasn't the one for me and once I changed my routine, I found a really great guy."

The **AVERAGE** Guy	Guys go to bars to find women they don't have to work very hard to sleep with that night.

Try Dating These Guys

While you're dating, remember to look for guys who fit your current criteria, not guys who are like the losers you used to date. If you focus on your past, you may let one of these seven guys pass you by. Who are they? They are the seven guys every single girl should date at least once in her life. They're perfect for rebounds!

7 GUYS Every Single Girl Should Date

1. **The workaholic**—every woman should date a guy who's got goals and works hard to achieve them. Sometimes you may run into a faux workaholic who uses the guise of gainful employment to fool you into thinking he's making money when, in reality, he's making out with another woman. That's not the kind of guy I'm talking about here. I'm talking about a guy who works hard and takes care of his responsibilities. If you run into a guy like this, hang on to him, because he's got the drive to go places (with you in tow!).

2. **The bookworm**—sure, guys who are into books are nerds . . . but they're also fountains of untapped knowledge who will hold your interest in a romantic relationship. Don't overlook the guy who keeps his head between the pages of a book and not between the legs of a stripper.

3. **The geek**—guys who qualify to be a part of the geek squad aren't necessarily that bad to date. On the contrary, geeks can often be fascinating men worth their weight in intellectual gold. As long as he doesn't sit in front of a computer playing video games all day instead of working, there's nothing wrong with giving a geek a shot at winning your heart.

4. **The cook**—if you're dating a guy who can cook, you might want to give the relationship a chance. It's rare these days to find a guy who can whip up a tasty meal for you on a consistent basis. And if he's home cooking for you, he's not going to have time to be out dishing his delicacies to another woman.

5. **The writer**—it used to be that guys who were into writing or poetry weren't seen as very macho. Oh, how times have changed! Writers are now viewed as the smart, but silent type. They've built a reputation for being sensitive and caring, so if you find one, give the union a chance to flourish. If nothing else, you may wind up with fabulous love poems written just for you.

6. **The green guy**—dating a guy who's into cleaning up the environment and cares about issues like global warming and the ozone layer can be a wonderful experience. So if you happen upon a handsome hunk determined to recycle and reduce his carbon footprint, don't dismiss him.

7. **The artist**—dating a guy who is into the arts can be fun, especially if he paints or sculpts. Artists can be sexy, because they're into self-expression and are thoughtful and creative.

You probably would never have even thought of dating guys like those listed above, but you should. Women are attracted to bad boys for a reason. Usually they're hot, tough, and sexy, with great bodies—everything a geek or bookworm is not. But bad boys will break your heart, every single time. You've watched many other women go through major love catastrophes at the hands of a heartbreaking bad boy. So give the others a chance!

How Long to Rebound

You shouldn't date your rebound for more than a month—two at the maximum. Get your practice, have some fun, and get out of there. Staying with a rebound guy too long can lead to a serious case of Broken Heart Syndrome and you don't want that, do you? Go out on a few dates with your rebound until you feel comfortable with your dating abilities. Are you still too nervous or shy around guys? Are you still not over your ex and can't stop talking about him? These are all signs that you need to keep dating rebounds until you're ready to test the waters and find a solid relationship.

Don't Settle for Mr. Right Now

Yes, dating can be brutal. There's no question about that. So far, you've read a lot of stories from women who've experienced all sorts of relationship trauma. To make matters worse, finding your prince can take a while, so you may have to be on the scene a little longer than you may have expected. Because of this, you might make a mistake that can be hard to recover from—settling for Mr. Right Now instead of holding out and finding Mr. Right.

Mr. Right Now may not be a great guy, but in your mind, he'll function quite well for a while. He'll fill the void in your life left by your ex. And although he may clearly be unqualified to be in the dating pool, much less a part of your love life, you keep him around just to avoid passing your time alone, or looking like a spinster who can't land a man. Maybe you're afraid of what your friends or society will think of you. After all, it's not cool for a woman to be unmarried and childless in today's society. If that's your predicament, you're widely viewed as having something wrong with you, which is absurd. And it's an unjust double standard—if a man were childless and unmarried, no matter how old he was, he wouldn't be viewed as a spinster.

Still, don't keep Mr. Right Now around to pass your time. You're not that desperate, honey! And you certainly don't have to believe that if you can't find a guy for a long period of time, you're ultimately destined to become a sulky spinster. "Often we stay in relationships that aren't right for us just so we can have a warm body around," says dating expert Alison James. "Remember—it is far better to be single than to be in a bad relationship. Don't settle. The time you waste on the wrong guy is better spent looking for the right one." You heard Alison! Don't ever settle for an inappropriate guy, especially a Mr. Right Now who you know you have no future with. Isn't your precious time worth way more than that? Spend your time with a guy who actually has a shot at winning your heart for all the right reasons.

Shop for a Brand-New Boyfriend

Time for Some Retail Therapy

Drop everything and listen up, young lady! We're going shopping, right now! But on this spending spree, you won't be scoping out a pair of sexy stilettos or a dazzling designer dress. Instead, you'll spend your time shopping for a brand-new boyfriend—someone you could date in a serious relationship. Now that you're done with Mr. Right Now, it's time to renew your search for Mr. Right. Shopping for a new guy might seem a little strange at first, but just think of it like walking into a store and finding the perfect pair of jeans calling out to you from the rack, "Buy me! Buy me!"

Once you spot them, you still don't know if they're going to be a good fit until you actually go into the fitting room and try them on. Once you do that, you may find that what you thought were the perfect pair of jeans really make your butt look big or they're a bit too snug around your waist. So you move on to another pair of denim that looks and feels fabulous on you. You try them on and everything looks okay, so you bite the bullet and buy them.

But when you take them home, it's evident that they just don't look as good as they did in the store's fitting-room mirror. What you need to find is a pair of jeans that are really gorgeous and good-looking, the kind that you'll keep for a long time because they are absolutely perfect when you put them on. They make your butt look great. Maybe you might have to alter them a bit because they're a bit too long, but in the long run you've reached your goal—finding the perfect pair of jeans that will be there when you need them and last you a long time.

Finding a new guy is a lot like that. You're essentially shopping for a brand-new man. And just like there are a slew of clothing brands to choose from that could possibly look good on you, you're going to meet all types of guys out there on your search for love. When you get started, you might find a guy who looks perfect on the outside, but after the first date, something inside tells you he's not Mr. Right. Or you really hit it off with a guy, but after a few dates, the sparks fizzle and it becomes clear he's not the one for you. It's no big deal, so don't get worried.

Remember, you're trying to find the perfect pair of jeans. They're not all going to fit just right like you want them to. If they don't fit, put them back on the rack and leave them there for the next woman who comes along, because they might be the perfect fit for her.

You'll Have to Try on a Bunch of Pairs

There isn't much you can do about the types of guys you'll find on the dating scene. They're out there and no matter what you do, you'll encounter cheaters, liars, and losers. It's inevitable, just like death and taxes. But the minute you know a guy isn't right for you, take him back for a refund and do the only thing you can do—keep shopping. Eventually, you will find the guy who is the absolute perfect fit for you in every way.

That's what happened to Holly, twenty-five. "When I tell you that I went out with a million guys before I met my husband," Holly says, "I really mean it. It seemed like I was on an endless roller coaster of dates and most of these guys shouldn't even have been trying to date in the first place." Holly encountered men with all kinds of issues—commitment problems, bad breath, and trouble paying the rent. "These guys were just looking for a woman to be a victim of their cons, a maid to pick up after them, or to give them a place to live rent free. It was just awful. I always wondered how some of these guys even had the audacity to put themselves out there on the dating scene."

But Holly didn't just encounter jerks or guys with problems. "I did meet a few really nice, well-put-together guys who would be perfect for a lot of great women out there," Holly says. "I didn't necessarily click with them, but I would definitely introduce them to my best friend or my sister." Eventually, Holly did find the guy who was her perfect fit and she didn't just date him, she married him.

So what advice would Holly give to girls who've got to get back out on the dating scene? "Don't stress it," Holly says. "Dating isn't a race to see who can get married the fastest or have a baby the quickest. It's a process, and you have to let it take its natural course. Relax and let love work its magic. You'll find the one. Don't worry."

Don't turn shopping for a new guy into a chore. Like shopping, dating is supposed to be fun, not work. So don't get too caught up in whether the guy you're going on a date with will make a good husband, or if he's a got a job that puts him on the fast track to becoming a millionaire. If there's a spark there, you'll find all of that out soon enough. For the moment, focus on the present and enjoy the moment you're in with him (and the food, too). Not every guy you date is going to be the perfect fit and, like a lot of other things in your life right now, you're just going to have to accept that. There's nothing wrong with you and there may be nothing wrong with him. It's okay. But the two of you just weren't the perfect fit for each other. It happens.

> **The AVERAGE Guy**
>
> Guys take the shopping approach to dating, but we also know we can always trade in our old merchandise for an upgrade if things don't work out.

Now, what strategies should a single girl like you employ to actually find the perfect guy that fits? First, you've got to become a savvy shopper. How can you shop for a great new guy unless you know how to do it the right way? You must also learn how to instantly spot guys who are damaged goods—men who lurk on the dating scene with more emotional baggage than you can fit in the storage compartment of a Boeing 747. And last, but certainly not least, when you've decided a guy isn't the right fit, you need to send him back to wherever it was you found him.

Become a Savvy Boyfriend Shopper

A girl who knows what she wants in a man won't waste time on guys she knows aren't right for her. In addition to your Don't Date Him, Girl list, you must know how to use your intuition, also called your Built-in Boyfriend Bullshit Detector. That's how you'll spot fake fellows on the dating scene who are out to break your heart. You'll also need to learn the various ways you can discreetly ditch a date you know isn't really right for you. On the dating scene, you'll find that some guys you date spew a lot of bullshit. They'll exaggerate the circumstances of their last breakup, fib about how much money they make, or otherwise make you think they're perfect when they're not. That's where your Built-in Bullshit Detector comes in. It's a handy tool for helping you spot the snakes slithering on the dating scene dressed like guys. It's that little feeling you get that tells you something isn't right. It's the voice in your head telling you that you might be making a big mistake. Listen to it.

You are now on your way to being a savvy shopper on the available boyfriend market. But besides realizing that you can't fix or change a guy, here are eight more things every single girl aspiring to be a savvy shopper must know!

> **The AVERAGE Guy**
>
> A woman isn't going to be able to fix a guy with flaws unless he really wants to be fixed and that's a very rare thing, so women shouldn't waste their time trying.

8 THINGS Every Savvy Shopper Should Know

1. **Don't fully commit to a new guy until you've met his parents, best friend, or someone who can vouch for him.** Sure, he may have told you about these people when you started dating, but you won't know exactly what the situation is until you've had a look for yourself. Before you give your heart to a guy, you want to get a good look at what you're committing yourself to if you decide to get into a relationship with him. That includes understanding his circumstances and getting to know the important people in his life. If you really like the guy and he doesn't bring up organizing a meet-and-greet with his fam, you can suggest it yourself. There's no harm in that.

2. **Don't accept an invitation to go out with a guy until at least twenty-four hours after he's asked.** You don't have to rush to say yes to a guy who asks you out. Take it slow, do a little research. Log on to DontDateHimGirl.com and search for his name, or Google him and see what comes up. Then accept his invitation if you find that he's worthy to share a little bit of your precious time. Lots of guys are going to ask you out, but the ones you want to give your time to are the ones who might make good long-term boyfriends, not fly-by-night flings.

3. **Don't date a guy who takes too long to call you back.** If you reach out to a guy, don't sit by the phone waiting for him to return your call. At the same time, however, when you call him, he should return your call the same day or the next day. If a guy takes a week to call you back, he's obviously busy with other things and isn't the right guy for you.

4. **Don't date a guy seriously until you know where he lives and you've seen his place with your own two eyes.** You can go out on, say, five dates with a guy before you see where he lives. After that, it's time to check out his crib. So many women date guys for long periods of time without knowing exactly where their guy lives. How could you share your time (and maybe even your body) with a guy yet not know where he sleeps every night? That doesn't make any sense. If a guy keeps the location of his place under wraps while your life is an open book, something's wrong.

5. **Don't date a guy who's always late for your dates.** Respecting the time of the guys you encounter on the dating scene is an essential part of being a good dater. If you've made a date with a guy, be on time. If he can't seem to give you the same respect, ditch him. Why would you want to date a guy who can't show up at a restaurant on time? If you get into a relationship with him, he will definitely be late for something important—just hope it isn't your wedding!

6. **Don't date a guy who talks too much about his ex.** You'll encounter guys on the dating scene who say they are over their ex and ready to move on, but in reality, they're just looking for someone to date while they try to get over her—*Ms.* Right Now. Don't let that be you when you're looking for long-term love! You can always tell a guy who's stuck on his ex by the number of times he brings her up. If he's constantly talking about her, instead of trying to get to know you, he's not ready for another relationship yet.

7. **Don't date a guy who spends too much time at work.** Ambitious guys are great, but if all the guy you're dating does is eat, sleep, and work, he's probably not really available for a serious relationship. He may not be doing anything wrong, but if you get into a relationship with him, you're hardly ever going to see him, and that's no fun.

8. **Don't date a guy who's too friendly with other women.** These guys are very easy to spot. They're the guys who ogle other women right in front of you with no remorse, or the guy who has to chat up every waitress, store clerk, and random woman in his vicinity. Then there's the guy in the gym who will see a woman using a particular piece of equipment and slither up to her to start a conversation by asking her if he can use it too. If you encounter a guy like this, definitely ditch him. He's so not the one for you! A guy like this can only bring you heartache if you decide to get into a relationship.

So now that you're on your way to becoming a savvy shopper, let's talk more about how to avoid the mistake of giving your heart to a guy who's damaged goods.

Don't Buy Damaged Goods

Many women have experienced the disappointment of buying something fabulous in a store that later turns out to be flawed. Don't make the same mistake with your love life. Committing your heart to a damaged man is like keeping defective merchandise bought in a store and trying to repair it yourself instead of doing what you know you should do: return it for a full refund.

You've only got a limited amount of time on Earth and you can't waste it with guys who are cheaters, liars, and losers. Surprisingly, many women don't actually realize this. Instead of spending their time looking in the right places for the right kinds of guys, some women would rather spend their time trying to fix, feed, or nurse a guy who clearly does not have his act together emotionally or financially.

Tracy, thirty-three, made the mistake of focusing on the needs and wants of a man instead of herself. She wasted three years of her life with a guy who cheated on her several times and lied throughout their entire relationship to cover his tracks.

"I thought my ex was a major jerk because he was cheating on me," says Tracy, "but at least I knew what to expect from him. I had him figured out. I didn't think I could handle leaving him and then dating someone new." Tracy was hesitant to try life without her philandering partner. She felt a certain comfort in knowing what her guy would do. She was too afraid to try her hand at a love life that didn't involve cheating, stress, anxiety, frustration, and pain.

"I thought if I got into a new relationship, I wouldn't know what I was in for with him because he would be new," Tracy says. "I played the *What If* game and decided I didn't want to take a chance of finding real love by leaving my ex for a guy I didn't know."

In addition to being afraid, Tracy was convinced that she could change her ex. "After trying over and over again to fix my ex and our relationship," Tracy says, "I realized it wasn't my job to make him an honest, loving man. He should have done that on his own. I was clearly wasting my time."

"Guys will continue to use you, cheat on you, and hurt you as long as you let them," warns the Average Guy. That's why you have to take charge yourself and refuse to be his mother, maid, or secretary.

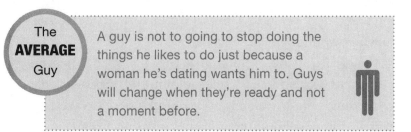

The **AVERAGE** Guy

A guy is not to going to stop doing the things he likes to do just because a woman he's dating wants him to. Guys will change when they're ready and not a moment before.

Sure, if you bought clothing that's ripped or otherwise damaged—you could whip out a needle and thread and fix it quickly. But it isn't so easy when you're saddled with a damaged man. While you have a sewing kit with needle and thread to fix torn clothing, there's no kit on the market today for repairing a damaged man.

ARE YOU DATING A DAMAGED GUY?

So how do you know the guy you're dating is damaged goods? It may not be readily apparent. He may not have any outward signs of damage, but when you scratch the surface and look a little closer, you can't miss it. To help you, here are eight signs you're dating a guy who is damaged goods.

➤ **He's badly in need of a repair that you can't possibly make.**
The guy you're dating doesn't just occasionally leave the

toilet seat up. Nope, your guy can't seem to hold a job, balance his checkbook, or be on time for a date with you. Ditch him. He's clearly damaged and you don't have the time to waste! Remember, your goal is not to find a man that you have to fix. It's to find a guy who's well-rounded and ready for a relationship. Don't waste your precious time trying to fix a guy who is clearly broken.

- **He's got a chip on his shoulder the size of a small state.** If the guy you're dating is walking around angry at the world because of something that was done to him in the past, he's damaged. He hasn't properly healed from whatever hurt was done to him. Instead, he just proudly displays it on his shoulder for the world to see. Don't date him, girl, because no matter what you do, you're never going to single-handedly knock that chip off. Only a therapist can help him do that.

- **He embellishes his accomplishments.** If the guy you're dating told you he was a scientist but really works as a night janitor at a medical laboratory, there's a huge difference there that you need to know about. If it seems like your guy is constantly exaggerating the things he's done or lies about what he's currently doing, he's damaged and needs help of a variety that you can't provide.

- **He's got an ego that just won't stop growing and it constantly needs to be fed.** It is one thing to be with a confident guy and quite another to be with a guy whose ego is bigger than a small country. A guy with an ego won't respect you. He'll think he knows it all and that your opinion really isn't relevant. If you've got a guy like this, he's damaged and will need extensive repair that you can't give him.

- **He's stuck with the ghost of a relationship past.** Sure, you can be friends with an ex, but if she seems to be your boyfriend's top priority, he's obviously damaged. If he's late for a date with you because he was talking on the phone with her, he hasn't let go of that former relationship. He is so stuck in the past with her that he can't see the present with you.

- **He can't keep his finances flush.** In a tough economy, everyone, women included, has money problems. But if the guy you're dating is consistently bouncing checks, late on his rent, and won't do anything about it, he's a damaged fellow who needs a credit counselor, not you as his girlfriend.

- **His bad habits are beyond belief.** If your guy can't stop giving his rent money to a stripper or guzzles gin in the morning and washes it down with wine and vodka in the afternoon, he's damaged with a bad habit you can't fix, so don't waste your precious time trying.

- **He puts you down.** Often, damaged people hurt others so they can feel better about themselves. It doesn't make sense, but it happens. If you're dating a guy who is constantly putting you down, however subtle his taunts may be, he's definitely in need of some help and you're not the one to give it to him.

CAN YOU FIX A DAMAGED GUY?

Sometimes you find damaged merchandise in the bargain bin. Every girl loves a bargain—a pretty purse at a deep discount, hot high heels that are 50 percent off, or a sexy slip dress marked down to nearly nothing. When it comes to guys, though, finding a bargain isn't necessarily a good thing. When you're out shopping, you'll find scratched and dented merchandise—damaged goods on sale. Those are the guys with problems that they need to solve on their own. Sure, they may be handsome or funny, but they're still damaged and you shouldn't bother trying to fix them, so don't commit your time to them.

The **AVERAGE** Guy

Damaged guys have damaged relationships. Instead of trying to date a guy with problems, leave him alone and move on.

Instead of rushing for that bin of bargain boyfriends, stay away—damaged goods aren't always what they appear to be. That tiny scratch on the outside could hide an even deeper cut underneath. On the dating scene, damaged goods usually show up in the form of unavailable guys who swear to you they indeed have all the free time in the world to devote to a relationship; commitment-phobic Casanovas who will date you for years, but never actually put that ring on your finger; and pathetic players who think it's okay to date you and several other women at the same time without anyone knowing it but him.

Don't be fooled into thinking that all damaged goods can be brought home and fixed. Sure, every woman would like to think that she's got the power to change a guy, but like the late actress Natalie Wood once said, "The only time a woman really succeeds in changing a man is when he's a baby."

Before becoming a savvy shopper, Angela fell for many cheaters, liars, and losers. "I just didn't get it," Angela says.

"If a guy was a jerk or a loser, you could almost bet that I would ignore the signs and fall madly in love with him anyway." Angela didn't know how to shop properly. Instead, she just kept making the same mistakes with men, dating damaged goods over and over again.

"It seemed like the guys I dated were all horribly flawed in some way, but I didn't notice because I was too busy being in love," says Angela. "Instead of running the other way when I met a guy, I was determined to be the one woman who could fix him and make him into the guy I wanted him to be." Eventually, Angela learned how to shop the right way and found a great guy whom she later married.

Remember: It's *Your* Time You're Wasting

You've read this phrase many times before throughout this book—don't waste your precious time. It's worth repeating because the message is extremely valuable. Don't spend those moments with a guy who isn't worth it. Don't be sucked in by a guy's sob story. We've all got something bad that's happened to us in life, and a decent guy wouldn't use his past traumatic experiences to try and pick up a date.

When you spend time trying to fix a broken man or give a cheating one a second chance, all you're doing is delaying your dating destiny. You can't find love because you're too busy wasting time trying to fix a jerk who isn't ever going to be the man you really want him to be.

After the third or fourth date, you'll know if you want to spend more time with a guy. If you've determined a guy you're dating clearly isn't the one, don't keep dating him. End the relationship with class and dignity and move on. You'll be doing yourself a huge favor in the long run. Don't think that you can stick with it for a while to see if you'll be the girl that changes him. Like the Average Guy said, guys don't change just for a girl.

If you get into a relationship that starts off well but you later realize it isn't going anywhere for whatever reason, do the same thing: end it. You don't owe anyone a certain length of time. Whether it's been three dates or thirteen, if it's not going anywhere, move on.

ASK YOURSELF: ARE HIS FLAWS REALLY DEAL BREAKERS?

Remember, there are no perfect people in the world, especially guys. No guy out there comes without flaws, emotional baggage, and other imperfections. And you aren't perfect, either. Just like the guy you're dating, you've got issues that need addressing and anger that needs resolving. The question you have to answer in a relationship, however, is whether or not those flaws your guy has are acceptable to you.

For example, there are some things that guys can't help. For example, it's one thing if the guy's a little short. He can't help that. Both Prince, who stands at five feet three, and Tom Cruise, at five feet nine, have been rumored to wear lifts in their shoes to compensate for their lack of height. But if the guy you're dating lies or cheats, there's really no easy fix for that. And you know from your list of important criteria that you have to focus on the more important features of a guy—his character, his loyalty, and his heart.

"Think of finding a guy like shopping for a new house," says the Average Guy. "If a guy's a fixer-upper and needs just a little bit of work, such as a new coat of paint, keep him, but if he requires a full remodel, look for another house." Why would you want to sink your precious time into a remodel when you can find a guy who just needs a little bit of work?

Keep the Receipt—You May Need a Refund

When you're shopping, it's important to keep your receipt for each purchase you make just in case you need to return whatever snazzy item you've purchased. The same thing applies when it comes to guys. Think of committing to a particular hottie like making a purchase, like when you commit to that brand-new Prada purse. You still have to take your merchandise home, inspect it, and see if it's really what you want to commit to it. Maybe in the store, the color was gray, but when you got it home and actually saw it in the light, it was really more purple, your most hated color. You have the chance to return it before wearing it.

Apply the same principle to the guys you meet. Sure, you can go out on a date or two, but don't fully commit to any guy too quickly. Use your Don't Date Him, Girl list for support. Remember, the consequences of committing too quickly in a relationship can be disastrous. Moving in with a guy too soon or merging financial forces too quickly can turn into a mess that takes a long time to clean up. Don't date as though you're in a rush and don't be afraid to listen to your intuition and return damaged goods. Take things slowly and cautiously with new guys you meet and at the first sign that he's damaged or that he's deceived you, run and don't look back. While you're wasting your time with a guy who isn't worth the effort, you're missing an opportunity to be with a great guy who deserves your time.

Should You Shop Online for a Great Deal?

You might think online dating is either a blessing or a curse, depending on how your experience looking for love in cyberspace turned out. If you and the guy you met online are poster children for one of those happily-ever-after eHarmony commercials, in your mind, online dating is awesome. If, on the other hand, you ended up getting swindled, cheated on, lied to, or otherwise traumatized by a cad you met in cyberspace, then you've got a very different view of dating via the world wide web, and it doesn't involve hearts, red roses, wedding bells, and sappy TV commercials.

> **The AVERAGE Guy**
>
> Most men date online because it allows them to paint a picture of themselves as perfect. These are the guys who lie in their profiles about their weight, job, or marital status. Don't be discouraged by those guys. Give online dating a try because for every liar lurking on an online dating site, there is one who is truly out there looking for a good relationship.

Kimberly, twenty-five, knows the downsides of online dating all too well. She dated a guy who used Internet dating sites to break hearts. "Women need to know that if you meet a guy online, chances are you're not the only one he's dating," warns Kimberly. "And if you choose to actually date a guy you met online, he may use the very same dating site he met you on to cheat on you by hooking up with other women on the site.

Kimberly's guy was using Match.com, JDate.com, and others to cheat on her. "He knows how to work the social networking. He admits to trolling and stringing ladies along. He dates several girls at a time and never tells them about each other."

PROS OF ONLINE DATING

Online dating has many pros. That's why millions of people around the world do it. It's convenient and easy to do. You don't have to leave the house to do it and it doesn't cost a lot of money.

"Online dating is one of the best inventions ever. What could be better than a searchable database of single men?" says Sonia Torretto, DontDateHimGirl.com's resident counselor. "The concept is brilliant. It is kind of like shopping online—there's a large selection and you don't have to waste hours driving from store to store to find the one you want. Of course, sometimes your purchase doesn't look exactly like it did in the picture, but it's still easy and fun. Many people have found the love of their life this way."

CONS OF ONLINE DATING

But it also comes with just as many cons. For one thing, there's the rampant dishonesty. In online dating, guys start off any relationship they get into on *their* terms. They can be whoever they want to be. There's also the fact that a lot of men use the Internet to troll for women to hurt, scam, or steal from. Take accused rapist Jeffrey Marsalis, for example. He used Match.com to find his alleged victims. In his online profile, he told multiple women in different states that he was a surgeon, astronaut, and a doctor, among other things. According to ABC News, "In April 2005, Jeffrey Marsalis was arrested and charged with multiple counts of rape. Philadelphia police said he had been using an online profile to meet women whom he would date, drug, and rape. Twenty-one women in the Philadelphia area told police that Marsalis had raped or sexually assaulted them, all of which he denied. Ten of these cases were prosecuted in two separate trials. His colorful profile included many pictures of him in various assumed identities, including a souvenir NASA photo, altered so that his name appeared on the nametag. His profile described his ideal woman: "If you want to be my copilot on the magic carpet ride, it's carry-on only, that means no stop signs, no stop lights, and throttle up."

Yes, this is an extreme example, but it shows you what's out there! So you've got to be on the lookout if you're going to date online. Keep your wits about you and remember, if a guy seems too good to be true, he probably is.

Online dating is also a haven for married men who want to convince you that they're single. Christy, twenty-seven, fell victim to a married dater.

"I dated a guy I met online for about three months," says Christy. "He swore over and over again that he wasn't married. When I finally got around to checking out his story, I found his marriage certificate and realized he was still with his wife and had no intention of marrying me like he said he did."

Christy was devastated, but you don't have to be. Online dating doesn't have to end in disaster, though. It can actually be a lot of fun. You may just end up in a commercial for one of those dating sites, too!

THE #1 SECRET TO SUCCESSFUL ONLINE DATING

As you can see, the main problem with meeting guys online is the possibility that they're lying to you about some aspect of their lives. So how do you protect yourself? *Do some research!* Don't date him, girl, until you check him out first. He may seem like Mr. Perfect in his online profile, but in reality, he's an unemployed, soon-to-be divorced bundle of baggage who isn't worth your time. Do your homework before letting a new guy you meet online share your precious time with you. Here's how to do it:

- **Log on to DontDateHimGirl.com to check out what other women might have to say about him.** DDHG has profiles of more than 100,000 men worldwide, so be sure to see if anyone has posted any information about your potential guy.
- **Google his name.** You can tell a lot about a guy from Google. Granted, not everything you find on Google is going to be accurate, but if he says he's a published author, you can easily find out from Google whether or not he's telling the truth.
- **Dig deeper.** Next, head to your local courthouse to confirm anything you find online. For example, maybe his Facebook profile says that he is divorced. If you can find the public records of the divorce in the courthouse, you'll know if there were any wrongdoings on his part that you need to be aware of (like abuse or cheating). Or, try Intelius or any of the other online background check services that are available. Most services will

do a background check for as little as $14.95, which is money well spent to save you future heartache. These searches will turn up arrests, property liens, and judgments against the guy, which you definitely want to be aware of.

*   **If you're lucky enough to be able to talk to any of his exes, by all means, do so.** It's a bold move, but a good one if you get the chance. Call her and tell her what you're trying to do. In the global sisterhood, most women will help you out by providing some perspective on the guy now that you're dating him. If you can, meet each other for lunch or grab a cup of coffee and chat. Ask her what happened in the breakup, how he is as a person, and what his flaws are. Most likely, you'll walk away better informed about the guy you want to date.

Doing research on the guy you're dating isn't weird or stalker-like; it's a necessary part of dating. In a world where cheaters, liars, and losers abound, you've got to protect yourself. Now comes an important question: Should you tell the guy you're dating that you're doing research? Sure! You can do it in a very forthright way. Tell him you've Googled him and talk about some of the fun things you found like his Facebook page or his LinkedIn profile. If he has nothing to hide, he'll welcome it. And if he is hiding something, you'll know soon enough by his protests.

Doing your research is the best way to see through a guy who's lying to you online. Here are four more ways to avoid the pitfalls of dating in cyberspace.

....

4 ESSENTIAL Rules for Dating Online

1. **Don't date a guy with a suspicious online profile.** Perfection isn't something the human race has been able to achieve. If his online profile seems just too good to be true, it probably is.

2. **Don't meet an online beau alone.** Sure, you may have had dozens of intimate telephone conversations and exchanged many heartfelt e-mails, but cheaters, liars, and losers use cyberspace as a playground for their sinister deeds. Whether it's hiding a marriage, dating many women at once, or telling a bold-faced lie that he's a millionaire, guys will use online dating to rewrite their romantic resumes. Since you really don't know who you're going to come face-to-face with, make sure to meet in a public place with a friend. Tell him you're bringing someone along so he can bring a friend too if he wants.

3. **Don't give up your goods in real life.** If you're going to meet guys online, you've got to guard your privacy. Make sure the men you meet online don't know your vital stats right off the bat. Keep your address, work location, and social security number under wraps at all times.

4. **Protect your profile password.** Don't give access to your dating profile to anyone, including a girlfriend. You want your privacy to be protected while you date online. Take charge by keeping your passwords in a safe place.

Whew! There's a lot to know about the dating scene today. Now let's make sure that you're meeting guys who are worthy of your fabulous self.

Date Smart!

Set Yourself Up for Success

You've come such a long way. Remember that sad, miserable girl who sobbed in her cosmo about her loser ex? She's in your distant past. Now let's talk about ways to give yourself the best chance at finding long-term love. You probably have lots of questions: *What kind of guy do I want to find? What if I'm afraid to date again? Where should I meet a good guy? How can I keep him once I've got him?* So many questions! Let's find the answers.

Decide Who You're Looking For

A smart dater knows what she wants. Do you? If not, it's time to figure that out so you can make intelligent dating decisions. Now that you're back on the dating scene for real, you need to revise your Don't Date Him, Girl list and add a column for the type of guys you want and don't want to date. List qualities or body types or anything you must have or want to avoid.

Okay, let's take a look at your list, shall we? If your top qualities in a man are bulging biceps and a nice car, but no mental muscle, you've got a problem. You've got to be realistic about what you're looking for in a man. That's what a diva would do. Why would you ever put muscles and a nice car on your list ahead of intelligence, gainful employment, and honesty? There are far more men in the world with muscles and tricked-out cars than there are with good, stable jobs and integrity.

Take a moment to revise your list (if necessary) by putting the superficial things like looks and how much horsepower he's got at the bottom of the list. Move things like character, kindness, and ambition up to the top. Doing this means that you have to decide what's really important to you. Is physical appearance really more important than his attitude? Looks can and will fade, so don't put vanity at the top of your list. But, be smart and make sure this list doesn't describe your last loser boyfriend in full detail. You don't want to end up with a version of the guy who broke your heart again, except in a different skin. That's what happened to Jocelyn's girlfriend.

"I met my girlfriend's new boyfriend over dinner one evening," says Jocelyn. "She was so excited to introduce me to him. When I met him, I determined he was just like her ex-husband but shorter." Jocelyn's girlfriend wasn't dating that way on purpose. She was just caught up in her own bad-boyfriend cycle. So, when she met someone who was just like her ex, she was instantly head over heels in love. That's not what a diva would do.

By arranging things in a realistic order, you'll remind yourself what's *really* important when you meet a guy. You'll be able to look past his long hair (he *could* get a haircut) and appreciate the fact that he loves his job as a second-grade teacher. You'll realize that it's okay if he drives an ancient car with 100,000 miles on it if he's saving money for a down payment on a house.

Find a Guy with Your Criteria

Okay, now that we've got that straight, let's talk about what to do when you meet a guy who has potential to meet some or all of the criteria on your list. As you get to know him, start looking at whether he has what you want. Compare the qualities he exhibits versus what's on your list, and put more emphasis on the important characteristics. Remember that you've got to be flexible. The likelihood is small that you're going to meet a man with every single quality outlined on your recently revised list. But if you're willing to be flexible and realize no guy is perfect, you will find a guy who has almost every quality on your list.

For example, let's say you wrote down that you don't want to date a guy with children. But then you meet a great guy with a little girl who you adore—are you really going to toss him aside just because you're sticking to your list? If you can be flexible about your "requirements," you might end up with a guy who has almost everything you're looking for, but throws a curveball into the mix too. It's okay to compromise in a healthy, mutually agreeable way that you feel comfortable with because of all his other great qualities. But you definitely *don't* want to compromise on certain deal breakers (never accept any cheating or verbal abuse, for example). No diva will change herself or what she deserves to get a guy.

Why is this list so important? Just as Dr. Dobransky says: "Women who get into 'bad relationships' don't have as much a problem with some 'deficit' in themselves as they do spotting a guy who is a poor fit for them early on. I think many women beat themselves up needlessly about how and why they have such a difficult time getting out [of a relationship], when really it's just a need for more attention *early* before getting *in*." If you've spent time figuring out what you want in a man, you're setting yourself up for success.

Get in the Right Frame of Mind

When you transition from dating Mr. Right Now to looking for a guy who might be Mr. Forever, you need to be sure you have the right attitude. You might have found it pretty easy to date casually, but when it's time to get serious, you might feel negative or skeptical all over again. You might think that every guy you go on a date with will be a manly mess that you aren't willing to clean up. You know that's not true, so stop thinking like that, young lady! Be confident in yourself and in the changes you've made in your love life. Now that you've identified your bad-boy habit, you'll be more attuned to guys who share negative qualities with guys in your past. You've empowered yourself to avoid cheaters, losers, and liars and you have a better chance than ever of finding a great guy who deserves you.

Dating by Ages

Today's dating scene is mostly segmented into different age groups because people usually hang out with other people their own age. Check out the sections that follow and pay particular attention to the one about your own age group. This information will help you navigate as you swim along in the dating pool.

TWENTY-SOMETHINGS

The tech-savvy twenty-something set tends to date within their age range, using the Internet as a means to communicate with people, especially on social networking websites like Facebook and MySpace. The younger crowd uses these sites to schedule dates with potential paramours and find great places to go on the perfect date. "I can't imagine my life without technology and social networking," says Amanda, twenty-one. "I definitely use websites for dating and meeting new guys."

Many of the guys in this age group aren't really ready to settle down. In fact, the last thing on their minds is getting married, having a mortgage, and making babies. They're having too much fun with their BlackBerrys, Wii video games, and Facebook accounts to slow down their action-packed lifestyles for just one woman. Most men in this age group are also on the hunt for money and spend a lot of time making it.

"When some guys are in their twenties, they don't want to be saddled with just one woman, security, and kids just yet," says the Average Guy. "They still have a lot of life yet to live and often want to wait until their late thirties or early forties to make a real commitment to a woman."

THIRTY-SOMETHINGS

Thirty-somethings have had their fun with romantic relationships. They've dated, had lots of sex, and they've acquired responsibility along the way. Daters in this age range may already have one child (or more), a mortgage, and a separation or divorce under their belt. These daters aren't motivated by money and technology like their younger counterparts; they want security and children and are actively working on settling down.

Men in this demographic are tricky. You'll find about half of them thinking about having their first child and buying their first home—but the other half aren't looking for any sort of commitment at all. They would rather spend their time pretending to be twenty years old without a care in the world.

FORTY-SOMETHINGS

Forty-and-over daters are more laid back. They've done a lot of living and a lot of dating. They've probably been through their fair share of divorces, separations, and bad breakups. After going through a few bad relationships, the men in this set often revert back to the behavior they exhibited in their twenties and are happier playing the field than settling down. They've tried being the loyal (or perhaps not-so-loyal) husband and it didn't work. If you're dating within this age range, you may even meet some men who have tried it many times but couldn't keep a healthy marriage going.

"This group of men is a tossup," says the Average Guy. "You'll find a lot of them who want to settle down because they're getting older and don't want to spend their remaining days alone. But a lot of them want to run around town with a twenty-year-old. It just depends on the guy."

Where to Find the Good Guys

It's time to take out the pen and paper again to take notes! Where are all the good guys hiding? That's the million-dollar question so many women try to answer. There are the usual places where good guys congregate:

- At church and charity events
- With a friend who set you up on a blind date
- At your place of employment

And we already talked about the pros and cons of online dating on page 136. But there are a few other places DontDateHim Girl.com members suggest for you to meet date-worthy guys:

- **Get classy.** Take a class in a subject that interests you and check out the hot guys all around you. "I met my husband at a real estate lecture," says Colette, thirty. "I didn't think I would find the love of my life among a bunch of real estate agents and investors, but that's exactly where it happened. The great thing about meeting a guy at a class or seminar is that the both of you automatically have a common interest that connects you."
- **Drive him wild.** When you're on the dating scene, you've got to go where the boys are to actually find one. You probably won't find a guy sweating it out at your neighborhood morning Pilates class, but you will find one where there are loud engines and big tires. Cars and boys go hand in hand, so grab a girlfriend and head to an auto auction like Stacy, twenty-six, did. "I know, you've never thought

about finding love at an auction," Stacy says. "But after I had a series of bad breakups, it was time to think outside the box to find someone. You never know if you'll find the man of your dreams under the hood of a hot car while you're there."

↗ **Take your best shot.** Guys love golf. Who knows why, but they love hitting the tiny golf ball into the little hole. Turns out, DontDateHimGirl.com members love it, too! Even if you've never swung a golf club, you can learn. Take lessons once a week for just one month like Victoria, thirty-four, did. "A girlfriend of mine dared me to take golf lessons because the instructor was a friend of hers who was cute," says Victoria. "I didn't hit it off with the instructor, but I met a lot of other great guys, some of whom I dated and had a great time with."

↗ **Dress for success.** There's no law that says women can only shop in clothing stores dedicated to skirts, stilettos, and stockings. To find potential love interests, you can sashay into a men's clothing store and boldly check out not only the fashions, but the fellows, too! The better the clothes, the better the caliber of guy you're likely to meet roaming through the racks. Amber, thirty-one, bypassed a shoe sale at Macy's to visit a men's boutique when she spied a cute guy there. "I was at the mall and I spotted a guy in a men's clothing store," says Amber. "Of course, I had no real reason to be in there, but I went in and started browsing near the cute guy and told him I was looking for a cool shirt for my brother. I asked his opinion about a shirt I picked and he asked for my number. The next day, we ended up going out for coffee. It was a lot of fun."

Besides these ideas, visit other places in your neighborhood where the boys are—the local bowling alley, a shooting gallery, or a basketball court. Basically, look anywhere good guys are known to gather.

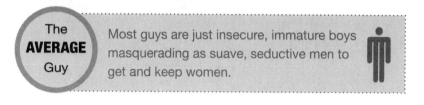

The **AVERAGE** Guy

Most guys are just insecure, immature boys masquerading as suave, seductive men to get and keep women.

Approaching a Guy

No matter what age or qualities you're looking for in a guy, you've got to be approachable when you're on the dating scene. That's what a diva would do. Think of it like meeting a new puppy for the first time without saying a word. When you get down on the floor and hold your hands out, the puppy understands that it is okay to approach you and give some needed love in the form of slobbery kisses. Without saying a word, you let the puppy know it can approach you and it won't get hurt. Men are the same way. They want to know that they can approach you without getting their feelings crushed.

DON'T OVERTHINK IT

When you're out on the dating scene, you're not looking to crush anyone. You're out there looking to fall in love with a guy who is right for you this time around. But you've got to give him a signal. Let a guy you meet know that he can make the first move without getting totally embarrassed. Here's a sample scenario to show you what I mean.

Let's say you're standing in line at a grocery store. As you're transferring your groceries to the conveyor belt at the cash register, you notice there is a hunky guy right behind you. You think he's pretty cute and better yet, he's not wearing a ring. You've taken a couple of glances his way and you notice that he's glancing back a little too. What do you do to let him know that you're approachable?

You look in his basket and figure out what you can talk to him about, of course! Ask him an open-ended question like, "Are those cookies as good as they say they are in the commercials?" He'll answer your question, you'll get to gaze at his cute face, and if you show a little initiative, chances are high that you'll score a date or at the very least his phone number. All he may have been looking for when he saw you there in front of him was a good reason to strike up a conversation with you. By being approachable, you gave him one. Good for you.

Now, how do you approach a guy who's with a group of friends? Do you approach him or are you going to let a chance at true love pass you by because your potential soul mate has a few friends around? "Go for it! You're going to make this guy look like a stud when you approach him in front of his friends," says the Average Guy. "Just ask him a question, any question. If he's interested he'll ignore his friends and find a way to keep you talking to him."

DON'T FORGET TO SMILE

Another thing you can do to keep your inner diva on display is to smile more. That's what a diva would do. Flashing your beautiful smile shows that you are an open person and is another great way to let a guy know that you are approachable. A sexy smile is one of the first things a guy notices on a woman. If you want guys to stay away from you, walk around with a frown on your face, instead. You'll notice that no one of the male species will approach you because they think you're either mean or in distress. A guy is not going to want to get involved with a woman who's either one.

When you smile directly at a guy, it's an unmistakable invitation that you're interested. Guys are just as shy and timid as women are when it comes to dating, so providing this kind of clear sign to a guy that you're definitely up for at least a little conversation is great.

What if you smile at a guy and he doesn't smile back? Don't despair. That's not what a diva would do. If you smile and look him in the eye and he doesn't respond, then he is either not interested or not available. Keep looking!

What Can You Do to Make It Work?

So, is there anything a woman can do to make a guy faithful and committed to a long-term relationship? Nope! Sometimes, even if you do everything the dating experts tell you, the relationship might end and there's nothing you can do to change that. But here are some great tips, and see Appendix A (page 227) for many more!

6 WAYS to Make Sure Your Guy Feels Happy and Loved

1. **Set the captive free.** Men hate feeling like they're confined to a relationship against their will. When they feel restricted, most men will stray. So if your boyfriend wants to go out with the guys one day, do the following. *(Yes, you can do it! Take a deep breath and practice.)* First, tell him to have a good time. Then, on his way out the door, grab him and whisper in his ear the many sexy things you'll do to him when he comes home. A man whose girlfriend does this will appreciate her because she gives him his coveted freedom. Men who get their freedom generally won't do anything to mess it up!

2. **Don't skimp on sex.** Women who have transformed their men into monogamy masters report that keeping the sex front and center in a relationship was one of the main reasons they have stayed faithful. Buy lingerie that will wow him, keep your body fit, and be adventurous in bed. He'll stick close to home if you keep it sexy.

3. **Stroke his e-spot.** Men love it when women stroke their e-spot. They love to hear it when we boost their egos by telling them how great they look, how sexy they are, and how skilled they are in the sack. Remember, you're the one your man wants to hear this from! Be sure to tell him often.

4. **Declare him innocent unless you can prove he's guilty.** Don't *ever* accuse a guy of cheating unless you're absolutely sure. Remember, woman's intuition is Mother Nature's way of giving us a head's up that something might be wrong in our relationship, but it's up to us to go out and

get the proof. A man who's constantly accused of cheating is going to become resentful of the woman who's accusing him, particularly if he's not actually cheating. But if you get proof of infidelity, feel free to confront your guy armed with it. Until then, though, keep the accusations to yourself!

5. **Go on an adventure.** Every once in a while, do something wild with your guy that will get his heart racing. When he least expects it, surprise him with something you know he'll love—tickets to a sporting event, dinner at his favorite restaurant, or a weekend away.

6. **Make him feel like a superstar.** Make sure you make your guy feel great every single day. After all, that's what you'd want from your boyfriend, right? According to marriage counselor Gary Neuman, author of the book *The Truth about Cheating*, 92 percent of affairs had by men aren't primarily about sex. Most men are looking for affirmation or appreciation from other women because they're not getting it at home. Make sure you compliment your guy and tell him how appreciative you are of the things he does for you.

Take Your Time!

When you get back into the dating scene, do it slowly. Don't go roaring back in like you're in college. If you meet a man with potential, rushing things could spell disaster for any hope of a future romance. Once you've gotten your feet wet in the long-term dating pool and had a few successful dates, you can start expanding your search for your Mr. Right.

Dating gets easier the more you do it. You'll also sharpen your skills at spotting a guy who clearly isn't right for you even before you sit down at the table for your first date. So don't avoid it, embrace it! Be sure not to lose the fierce, sexy woman who lives inside you. You may not feel like it right now, but you are a diva—dazzling, intelligent, virtuous, and accomplished. Inside of you is everything you need to be a confident woman who can strut herself on the dating scene with flair!

Also keep in mind that divas don't date more than one guy at a time and they don't settle down too quickly. Since you've just gotten back into the long-term dating scene, you should probably date a few Mr. Right Now types before settling down into another committed relationship. Just don't try to move in with or marry them. You're just getting back out there again after being in a relationship for a while, so you can't make a fair evaluation of your potential love prospects until you've auditioned a few of them.

If you've ever looked for a house or an apartment of your own, you probably remember falling in love with many different houses every time you went out looking. This is the way it is in the dating world, too. You have to see what's out there before you can make a fair evaluation of all the options that are available to you. Just take your time and look. After all, this is one of the most important decisions in your life. And please, please, please follow the rules.

Your inner diva is going to help you get back on the dating scene with class and confidence. She is a bold, beautiful woman who can have and do anything she wants if she puts her mind to it. Never let go of what she represents. Treat her with respect and show her the love and care she needs to keep helping you.

If your inner diva keeps you from dating just one bad guy, then it's worth it! She is that sweet little voice inside of you telling you not to call that jerk back or e-mail the loser who cancelled a date on you at the last minute. Listen to her—she should be on high alert when she reads about the losers in Step 8!

Avoid These Losers on the Dating Scene

Don't Date Jerks and Gigolos, Girl

The dating pool is infested with jerks and gigolos. Those guys care only about themselves and think of a single woman not as a lover or companion, but as a maid or meal ticket. Now that you've committed to avoiding these losers, let's make sure you know how to spot them before you get in too deep. This is no easy task—jerks and gigolos often come in shiny, deceptively wrapped packages—but you can do it. On the surface, they look great. They're hot, sexy, well dressed, and well mannered. They give off an air of prosperity and charm. Until, of course, you actually date one of them. If you meet a guy like this in your romantic travels, don't get distracted by his good looks or the hot car he drives. Material things don't make a relationship, engagement, or marriage work.

Sometimes it's hard to tell at first if a guy you're dating is a jerk or gigolo. When you first start dating a guy, he seems damn near perfect, but keep your eyes peeled, because he may not be what he seems. Here are ten signs you're dating a jerk!

....

10 SIGNS You're Dating a Jerk or Gigolo

1. **He is an eCasanova.** Watch for guys who use today's assorted technology and latest devices and gadgets on the market, not to stay informed about current events or work, but to juggle the many women that are a part of his life. An old-fashioned Casanova would probably just stick to the telephone or text messages to communicate with his mistress, but an eCasanova adds IMs, webcam, and the most current wireless devices to his arsenal of weapons, giving him the ability to manage his many lady loves with ease.

2. **He is self-centered.** Does he have a profound lack of caring or concern for other people? Does he think that the world revolves around only him? Well, my dear, bad news—he's a jerk!

3. **He can't keep his mouth shut.** Does he rarely ever censor himself? Does he says whatever is on his mind, even when the things he says hurt you? Jerks only care about themselves, so the feelings of others, including the women they date, aren't their top priority.

4. **He gives it to you straight, a little too straight, even when you don't ask him to.** Only a true jerk would bluntly tell you on the first date that he wants to bed you. That's because a jerk only cares about himself and his need and when he meets you, his only need is a casual, meaningless romp in the sack with no strings attached.

5. **He doesn't care what you think.** Does he have a habit of giving you "it's my way or the highway" ultimatums? Characterized by their lack of caring, these guys don't want you to have your own opinion or to voice it.

6. **He thinks your initials are ATM.** A gigolo will attempt get his hands on your money before he even tries to get you into bed. He'll tell you about the bad things that have happened to him and why he needs money from you to solve his problems. If it seems like the guy you're dating is a walking hard-luck sob story, don't stick around to listen.

7. **He wants to marry you faster than you can say wedding.** There are so many women who have been duped by gigolos who put pressure on them to consent to a quickie wedding. Don't marry any man before you've dated him for over a year, checked him out financially (that includes running a credit report; more on that later), and checked his bank balance before you even think about merging your finances with his.

8. **He wants you to cater to him.** Does he suffer from a chronic case of broken hands? You would think his hands were broken because he can't do anything for himself. The only thing is, he doesn't wear a cast. Don't date that kind of guy. You're no man's maid or secretary!

9. **He isn't reliable.** Jerks and gigolos have a habit of not being able to keep their word. They will make plans to take you out on a date and then break them at the last minute after you've already gotten all dolled up. These kinds of guys don't do this to you just once; they do it over and over again, leaving a trail of your hurt feelings behind them.

10. **He cheats.** Both jerks and gigolos cheat often. When you realize you're not the only woman with a spot on a guy's dance card, call it quits and move on. You've got a broken heart to heal and can't waste time resuscitating a long dead former relationship with a philanderer.

Get Fooled

...ost women, you've probably dated a few guys you'd rather forget about. We've all been there, girl! Many of the most intelligent women in the world have given their hearts to well-dressed wolves masquerading around in stylish (or not stylish) men's clothing. Whether you've dated a married father of two who told you he was single or a jobless jerk who told you he was wealthy, many women just like you have run into bona fide bad guys and believed their lousy lies.

So how do we miss the signs? Why do we end up kicking ourselves later for not realizing what these guys were really like? Here are some reasons:

- **You want to believe him.** Many of us simply want to see the good in people and don't want to walk around suspicious of everything a guy says. You're looking for a nice guy, and you want to believe you found one.
- **You make excuses for him because you don't want to be alone.** I've mentioned this before. If you're afraid to be alone, you may ignore red flags or make endless excuses for a guy's misbehavior. Part of getting over your bad habit of dating losers is catching yourself when you do this.
- **You're a sucker for a fix-it job.** Even if you see flaws in a guy, you may think you can help him change his ways. Unfortunately, this rarely works, and you have better things to do with your time!

Since you *know* by now that you can't continue to date these jerks and losers, let me tell you how to identify and avoid the most common types now that you're dating again.

Liars

Sadly, liars are all too common on the dating scene. A liar is someone who's dishonest about anything, large or small. Faith, twenty-three, met a liar. She couldn't tell the truth from the lies when it came to her ex-boyfriend, a guy she came very close to marrying.

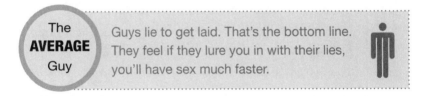

The **AVERAGE** Guy

Guys lie to get laid. That's the bottom line. They feel if they lure you in with their lies, you'll have sex much faster.

"Among the many things that he lied to me about were his age, where he lived, and how much money he made," says Faith. "He created a persona of the perfect guy, made me fall in love with it, and continued to tell me one lie after the other."

HOW CAN YOU TELL IF A GUY IS LYING?

Faith wasn't able to spot her ex-boyfriend's lies until it was too late, but you don't have to suffer the same fate. Here are two ways that experts say can help you spot a liar.

↗ **Listen to what he doesn't say.** In a 2008 CNN.com article, Dr. Paul Ekman, a University of California professor and the author of *Telling Lies: Clues to Deceit in the Marketplace, Politics, and Marriage*, says, "Liars hate to give detail and often are evasive. Though con artists normally rehearse their lies and may look completely at ease answering your questions, ask for a lot of specifics. It will be difficult for them to remember what they told you, and they'll eventually trip themselves up." So ask your guy for specifics!

↗ **Read his lips.** According to "The Body Language Lady," Patti Wood, pursing your lips inward and sucking them in "can indicate extreme anxiety, withholding information, and withholding aggression. Tight lips indicate you may be planning to keep the truth in." So look at your guy's lips when he talks to you about something to see if he might be fibbing.

THE LIES HE TELLS

Now that you know *when* he's lying, let's take a look at the kinds of lies he tells.

"Guys tell whatever lie is going to get them out of whatever trouble they're in with their girlfriends or wives," says the Average Guy. "That's one of the reasons it's so hard for women to tell a guy's lies from his truths." The Average Guy advises women to be on the lookout for the following fibs.

··

6 LITTLE Lies that Guys Often Tell Women

1. **"My ex broke my heart."** It's a fact that women can be just as bad as guys in romantic relationships. Women

cheat and lie just like men do, but if you encounter a guy whose entire dating resume comprises a string of different women who've broken his heart, take heed. He may have done a little breaking along the way that he's not telling you about.

2. **"I'm separated from my wife."** A smart, sexy, savvy woman like you does not date men who are attached to other women in any way, particularly by marriage. Don't fall for this lie no matter how cute the guy is. Separation from a spouse is not divorce by any means. He may be living in a different house or apartment than she is, but they're still very much married.

3. **"I'm getting a divorce."** If he's getting a divorce, he shouldn't be dating. Sheesh, wait a few months until the ink is dry on the divorce papers before you hit the dating scene. If you meet a guy who tells you he's in the midst of the divorce, tell him to call you when his divorce is finalized and then perhaps you'll think about dating him. Don't ever give your heart to a man who is technically married.

4. **"I haven't slept with a lot of women."** Sure, and the sky is really a gorgeous shade of red. Unless he was a monk or clergyman prior to meeting you, he's probably slept with quite a few women. By the time he was thirty, he could probably count them all on two hands and a few toes, but by the time he turns forty, he's going to need your fingers and toes to help him keep count. You'll never find out exactly how many he's had a roll in the hay with, but if he tells you he can count the number of women he's slept with on one hand, he's probably lying.

5. **"I don't have any kids."** There's a big difference between a guy not having any kids *living with him* and having no kids *at all.* Just because the kids don't live with him doesn't mean they don't exist. And if you don't want to be saddled with a guy who's got children, you've got to clarify exactly what a guy means when he says there are no kids in his life. It would seem like an easy question, but you would be surprised how many guys lie about having little ones.

6. **"I don't cheat."** There *are* guys out there who've never cheated on a woman they've dated, but those guys are rare, like flawless pink diamonds. A woman who lands a guy who's genuinely never cheated is truly lucky indeed. For the rest of you, when a guy utters those words, beware. You've also got to be really clear with your potential suitor about his definition of cheating. For example, most men don't think getting a lap dance from a stripper while you're in a relationship is "cheating," whereas most women would flag that as foul cheating behavior.

Cheaters

Speaking of cheaters . . . one of the most popular things girls dish about on DontDateHimGirl.com is why men can't just bite the bullet and be monogamous. They ponder ways to cure that nasty infection called infidelity that infiltrates their seemingly fabulous relationships with men. The women who use DontDateHimGirl.com need valuable dating advice and help with problems, such as what to do when they discover their guy has a girlfriend in cyberspace, or that he went on online dates and had long, passionate nights of cybersex. Or what to do when they find their man making moves on a female coworker; and then there's the poor girl who walks in on her prince and another woman in the sack. Yuck!

When you're dating a guy exclusively, you do so with the understanding that neither one of you is going to see other people. Cheating is not supposed to be part of the equation when you're dating exclusively. But what if the guy you're dating doesn't follow the rules? How would you know he's cheated?

Getting cheated on by the guy you have feelings for hurts like hell. And if the bastard who broke your heart is your fiancé, husband, or living with you, the pain of his betrayal can be even more painful to bear. As a woman, you might have been taught to turn the other cheek and just accept the tired, worn-out "boys will be boys" excuse. Or, you might have run like the wind the first time a guy you date sticks his manhood into another woman and lies to you about it. Either way, when a man you thought was monogamous turns out to be an avid adulterer, it sucks!

So why can't men just keep their manhood in their pants? It sounds easy enough, right? What makes it so hard for them to stay faithful to just one woman? The truth is—no one really knows for sure! But speculation about men and monogamy abound. The advent of Internet dating, online porn, and cyber-sex has further complicated matters of the heart. Check out these signs to protect yourself!

....

s Your Sweetheart Has Strayed

1. **He's missing.** If your guy seems missing in action from your relationship, he could be spending that time with another woman. Just ask pro golfer Tiger Woods' wife. Some of his alleged affairs occurred while he was partying in Las Vegas and she was at home in Orlando with their two kids.

2. **He's building muscle.** If your guy has suddenly taken a newfound interest in his looks, he's doing it for a reason. It's either he wants to look better for you or for another woman. Ask him about his new love for the gym. If he says he's doing it for you, great. If he's not, time will tell and it will soon become apparent whether or not he's cheating.

3. **He's keeping secrets.** If his life used to be an open book and now he's being secretive, something's up. Test him by grabbing his cell phone one day. If he panics and tries to snatch it away, he's got something on it he doesn't want you to see, such as a text message from another sweetie.

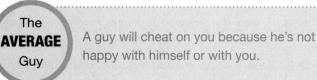

The **AVERAGE** Guy

A guy will cheat on you because he's not happy with himself or with you.

THE REAL STORY ON MEN AND MONOGAMY

Maybe men can't be faithful because they truly only love two things in life—sex and the women they want to have it with. It's not exactly earth-shattering news that men love to make love, but you probably would be shocked that your man thinks about sex in some way—fellatio, fornication, French kissing, and other assorted sex acts—literally every minute of the day. With all that sex on the brain it's no wonder men have little room in their heads to ponder the principles of monogamy. And, let's face it, ladies—men's little heads are often occupied by sexual urges that arise. You get the picture—men and monogamy often don't mix!

6 IMPORTANT Things You Don't Know about Men and Monogamy

1. **Men can feel the faith.** That's right, ladies! It's possible for men to be faithful. If a man really wants to, he can be with one woman for the rest of his life. So, why don't more men do it? Well, because . . . keep reading.

2. **Men freak out from the fear.** Men are afraid to fall in love with just one woman. They fear the unknown: how love will affect their bodies; what they're going to have to give up to fall in love. So to avoid having to deal with the fears that comes with being faithful, some men simply change women like they change their dirty socks.

3. **Men actually crave monogamy.** Monogamy is good for men and they know it, *but they would never admit it!* Monogamy helps men settle down and forge a productive, fruitful life. As they say, a little monogamy every day keeps the relationship drama away!

4. **Men have technology to make cheating easy.** It is really tough keeping up with a slew of different women, but with the advent of social networking, Facebook, and MySpace, they can actually do it. These men don't realize it's easier

to be faithful to one woman than to deal with the drama that juggling multiple loves will inevitably cause.

5. **Most men feel like they'll find a woman better than you.** A lot of guys don't really want to cheat on their lady loves and hurt them. They do it because they believe someone better is just around the corner. They want to get off the dating roller coaster and find the one woman who makes them happy once and for all, but they don't want to do it until they've exhausted all possibilities. Like many women, fear sometimes holds them back and prevents them from living a life of monogamy to its fullest.

6. **Men can't decide which woman makes him monogamous.** It's hard for some men to narrow down their dating prospects to just one woman—the one woman they're going to give their monogamy to. They may see the benefits of several different women and want to enjoy all their good qualities at once.

REASONS SOME MEN ARE ALLERGIC TO COMMITMENT

To many guys, *commitment* is a dirty word. It implies a loss of freedom, newfound responsibility, and wallowing in a sea of boredom. Some men are allergic to commitment and here's why:

- **Commitment cramps a guy's lifestyle.** When a man feels this way about commitment, he's going to keep his dating options open. "Some guys feel like they're missing out on something if they commit to just one woman," says the Average Guy. "They want to keep their options open at all times because they feel like they might find a woman who is better than the one they're dating."

- ✦ **Commitment isn't natural.** Men like this point to scientific evidence that suggests it's not natural for men to be committed to just one woman. Unfortunately for us women, just as there are facts to support the theory that men crave monogamy, there are also facts to support the theory that monogamy isn't natural. Some scientists insist men are genetically programmed to procreate with as many women as they physically can. Some scientists say that even when a man *wants* to settle down, he can't! Yeah, right! I'm not buying that one! What about you? If you encounter a guy who thinks that his purpose in life is to sow his seed with every woman who comes his way, he's definitely going to be allergic to commitment.

- ✦ **Commitment causes cheating.** A guy struggling with commitment is probably not getting what he wants from the woman he's with so he decides to test the dating waters by doing the breast stroke with another woman. "Happy men commit and don't cheat," says the Average Guy. "If there's something missing from a guy's relationship at home, he's going to look elsewhere to find it even if that means he has to cheat to do it."

- ✦ **Commitment = Boredom.** Men who think this way believe that if they commit to a woman, they will eventually get bored and restless in the relationship. "When guys get bored, one of the first things they look for to fill their time is sex," says the Average Guy. "They want to do something fun, but something they think is harmless, and so they log on to a porn site for a quick peek at a naked woman or flip through *Playboy* for a glimpse of a woman's breasts and it soon becomes the thing they turn to when they don't have anything else better to do. To them, it's better than focusing on commitment."

- ⚑ **Commitment isn't cool.** From the time they're little boys, most guys are taught that if you want to be seen as cool in the eyes of other men, you've got to have a bevy of beauties on standby. And you've got to have sex with as many of them as you can. This fosters a male culture that tells men that commitment is for cads and being on a merry-go-round of women is the right way to go. "Men are made to believe that sleeping with or dating a lot of women instead of committing to just one is a badge of honor," says the Average Guy.

- ⚑ **Commitment = No Control.** Cursed with a burning desire to have sex with everything that moves, men like this don't commit because they have a profound lack of self-control in the lower half of their bodies. "Just look at the actor David Duchovny," says the Average Guy. "He was in a committed relationship with his wife but couldn't control his need for other women and blew the commitment out the window."

So what's a single girl to do? You can run, hide, and never let another man within ten feet of you. Sure, this is certainly a safe way to avoid getting your heart broken again, but let's face it, girl—life without the company of cute guys will bore you to death, not to mention make it impossible for you to have sex! We can't have that now, can we? Luckily, when you understand why a guy cheats and learn what you can do to prevent it or detect it, your chances of being with a monogamous man are greatly increased. And your ability to spot a cheating man before he infiltrates your life will be sharper, too!

Okay, so now you know what men really think when it comes to monogamy and being faithful to just one woman. This knowledge will come in very handy when you're out there dating guys. You can tell a lot about a guy by the way he behaves in past relationships and if you think the guy you're dating has a history of infidelity and breaking hearts, you'll know it soon enough. Again, the key is to be honest with yourself and with him—be sure he knows your definition of cheating and that you won't tolerate it, and don't ignore red flags when you see them.

> **The AVERAGE Guy** Men will be faithful to the woman they feel they simply can't live without.

Fakers

Some guys on the dating scene aren't who or what they appear to be. The American actress Sharon Stone once said, "Women might be able to fake orgasms. But men can fake whole relationships." It's true! On DontDateHimGirl.com women post stories about being fooled by fake men all the time. These men are obviously liars, but they take the lying a step farther and can adopt fake personas just to reel women in. That's what happened to Genevieve, twenty-four. She was in a relationship with a guy for over six months and he turned out to be nothing like his fake persona.

"That was the worst relationship I ever had," says Genevieve. "He came across as just perfect, with a warm heart, a good personality, and a genuine love for me." But Genevieve's ex wasn't an honest, loving man. He was simply a good actor. "It turns out that I wasn't the only woman he wanted to spend his time with," Genevieve says. "While he was romancing me and had me convinced he was so great, he was wining and dining other women behind my back. It was awful."

Genevieve later found out her ex didn't own his own home; he really lived with his brother. He didn't own his own business; he worked for his father. "Almost everything he told me in the end was a lie," says Genevieve.

DON'T BE FOOLED BY A FAKE

So how do you know your guy is a fake? It isn't easy—some guys are really good at it. Check out these can't-lose signals.

....

7 KEY Signs to Spot a Fake

1. **He doesn't take you to his house.** If the guy you're dating has a problem taking you to the mansion he told you he lives alone in, most likely, he's faking his single status and really has a girlfriend or wife at home. Or his "mansion" is a run-down studio apartment in the wrong part of town.

2. **He doesn't have reliable transportation.** If your guy claims his car is in the shop, but it's been there for six months, he's probably not telling you just how challenged he really is in the transportation department.

3. **What he does for a living is suspicious, at best.** If your guy claims he's in the music industry but can't name the record company he works for and doesn't have any clients, he's probably faking his status as "an accomplished

record producer." And if he gave you the impression he once worked at the White House, but it turned out he really worked at the Waffle House, he's a fake and not the guy for you.

4. **He doesn't know his own name.** If the guy you're dating asks you to sign for something for him in your name, he's not the guy for you. Don't ever cosign for anything, like a car or apartment, for a guy, ever—under no circumstances shall you put your name on anything for any man that you're not legally married to. If your guy can't sign for something in his own name, you don't want the headache of being in a relationship with him. He's obviously got credit problems and that's something you don't want any part of.

5. **He lies about where he went to school.** If the guy you're dating has led you to believe he is an alumnus of the Ivy League but the only diploma on his wall is a GED from a vocational school, he's not a guy you want to be with.

6. **He isn't as well traveled as he told you he was.** If the guy you're dating made it seem like he traveled the world before he met you, but he's actually only seen it on TV because he's never left his hometown, he's a fake.

7. **He tries to tell you he's a Navy Seal or in Special Ops.** If your guy told you he was a Navy Seal or member of Special Ops, but he isn't even a member of his company's health insurance plan, he's not the guy you want to spend your future with.

Watch for these signs in the guys you date, and you'll catch most of the fakers out there before they hurt you.

Players

So what's the difference between a cheater and a player? Simple! A cheater is a guy who will carry out his desires to be with another woman. A player is a guy who wants women to "believe" he's got many women after him because he's so cool, hip, or handsome. He can be in a monogamous relationship, but he needs the attention he gets from other women to make himself feel better. So he'll do things that will take him right to the edge without actually cheating. For example, a player will date you, but if he spots a woman in a store, he'll talk to her and get her number but will never actually call her. He knows he's in a relationship with you, but he just needed that extra ego boost he got from the woman in the store handing over her digits.

To help you, here are six signs your prince could really be a player.

6 SIGNS Your Guy Is a Player

1. **He's got way too many phones.** If you notice that a guy you're dating has two or more different cell phones, it should raise a red flag right away. "When I was dating, I had two cell phones," says The Average Guy. "One for the women I wanted to date and one for my girlfriend."

2. **He's got too many e-mail addresses.** If your guy has a bevy of e-mail addresses for different purposes, beware. "Sometimes guys use different e-mails for different girls," says the Average Guy. "They want to keep the women separate and using different e-mails is one way to do it."

3. **He's dating online.** If you've been dating a guy for three to six months and he's still got a profile on a singles dating site, beware. Players like to leave the profiles up on sites like Match.com and eHarmony just in case things don't work out with the girl they're dating. Online dating profiles are very easy to find. To know for certain if your guy is dating in cyberspace, become a member of the dating sites in question and check it out for yourself. Although he may be dating you, he craves the reassurance that other women still find him attractive.

4. **He's homeless.** If the guy you're dating hasn't invited you over to his house within a month of dating, he could be hiding something. "Guys who are juggling multiple women don't want all of them to know where they live," says the Average Guy. If you've been dating for over a month and you still don't know where your guy lives, dump him.

5. **He's got more females friends than male ones.** If your guy boasts a slate of "best buddies" who are all women, he may be the type of guy who needs to validate his existence through his many female acquaintances and therefore, he's likely to cheat. This goes for his women friends in cyberspace also. If your guy doesn't want to change his relationship status on social networking sites like MySpace or Facebook to reflect that he's dating you, ditch him for a guy who is proud to let his friends know he's with you.

6. **He's a fan of finding love online.** If the guy you're dating has the online porn perusing habits of Christie Brinkley's ex Peter Cook, he's probably a player, too. The Internet is great, but it's got its downsides and the advent of Internet

porn is one of them. It's so easily accessible that guys, even married ones and guys in relationships, log on every day to meet and check out women having sex. If a guy is in a committed relationship and he's supplementing your sex life with porn and other women, he's gone too far. And while a little porn here and there is healthy for your sex life, it shouldn't completely *replace* it.

If you find yourself dating a guy who exhibits signs of being a player, do yourself a favor and leave. Pursing a romantic relationship with a player is a prescription for a broken heart.

Married Men

Believe it or not, married men masquerading as singles can be tough to spot. They will either lie to you about being betrothed or be brazen and wear their ring while attempting to date you. You should never, under any circumstances, date a married man, and before you give a guy your heart, make sure he isn't one of these six married masqueraders.

··
6 MARRIED Masqueraders Lurking on the Dating Scene

1. **The married "divorced" guy**—he's the married guy who will swear to you that he doesn't love his wife anymore and he's in the process of filing the paperwork to get a divorce. That could be true, but being the smart girl that you are, you aren't going to believe that until you actually see it. Tell him to take a hike till the deal is done.

2. **The married guy who's stuck**—this guy is married, but he tells you he doesn't love her and claims he won't leave her because of the kids they both share. That's nice that he's so loyal, right? But the fact that he's "stuck" in a bad marriage isn't your problem. "I was stuck in a bad marriage once and I did try to date women when I was both married and separated," says the Average Guy. "I, like most men who do this, just wanted to have sex with them while I was waiting on my divorce to become final."

The **AVERAGE** Guy

Married men hit the dating scene because they're bored. They don't want to leave their wives or significant others, but they want to have a little fun, too.

3. **The married guy with secrets**—this married man lurks on the dating scene and secretly dates other women behind his wife's back. Unbeknownst to those women that he dates, he's got a wife, kids, and a mortgage that he's not telling anyone about, including you. So if you get the feeling a guy you're on a date with is really married, ditch him quick! "There are a lot of guys out there who will date women and just blatantly pretend to be single even though they aren't," says the Average Guy. "In the end, it's the woman they're dating who gets hurt when she finds out he's got a wife at home."

4. **The married guy out looking for sex**—this is the guy who will tell you right away on the first date that he wants to have sex with you. That's because his only need is a

casual, meaningless romp in the sack with no strings attached and without revealing to you that he's married. Don't fall for it, girl! "My ex-wife was a terrible lover," says the Average Guy. "After being in that marriage over a decade, I couldn't take it anymore and started getting sex elsewhere. Women should not fall for a married guy who is doing this."

5. **The married man in need of a mistress**—this is the guy who will tell you right off the bat that he's looking for a mistress. He will make no bones about it and say it with a straight face. He's different than the previous guy because he wants a long-term sexual relationship with no commitment. If you encounter a guy like this, you know what to do. Run!

6. **The married guy looking for love**—this is the guy who will tell you he loves his wife but she's not meeting all of his needs or they've lost their emotional connection and he wants to have that connection with you. If you've made plans with a guy like this already, politely call and let him know that you're too busy to date him because you've got to wash your hair, shampoo your dog, or clean out your refrigerator. "Sure, a guy who tells you this is looking for something more," says the Average Guy. "It's called another woman."

When you meet a nice, unmarried guy, you'll recognize him right away. He'll be the guy who is exactly the opposite of the guys listed above!

Don't Date Like You're Dumb and Desperate, Because You're Not

Don't Be *That* Girl

There's nothing uglier than a desperate damsel out on the dating scene. She comes in many shapes and sizes, but one thing is readily apparent—she's desperate and making dumb decisions that mess up her relationships, or her potential for one. Now that you're committed to dating guys who are worthy of your attention, make sure you're holding up your end of the bargain. Don't be one of those women who is absurdly frantic to get a boyfriend, and don't commit stupid self-sabotage once you do snag a great guy.

You've seen her—the woman who calls lots of attention to herself by provocatively propping up her cleavage in a Victoria's Secret push-up bra and a sheer T-shirt for all to see—a "hey, look at me" gesture for all the gentlemen in the room. Granted, that desperate mating technique will attract a guy's attention, but he's not going to be the type of guy you want to take home to meet your mother. To get a guy's attention, you certainly don't have a second to spare parading around in clothing more suitable for a stripper than a savvy young woman like yourself.

There are other kinds of desperate women who don't flash their breasts to get noticed, but they've got different ways of oozing desperation. Think of the girl who just won't take no for an answer when a relationship ends. We've all had a girlfriend like this. Desperate for attention and affection from a former flame, she continues to find reasons, however inappropriate and idiotic, to maintain contact with him, even though he broke her heart.

"When guys see a woman who dates desperate they immediately wonder what's wrong with her," says the Average Guy. "We think they're defective because they are so desperate and they just don't get that a guy doesn't want to be with them anymore. Desperation is a sign that there is something wrong with this woman and that's why she's acting like she'll do anything and date anything just to avoid being by herself."

Why Do Women Date Desperately?

Why do women act like this when they date, anyway? Here are the two most common reasons.

THEY'RE AFRAID
Often, their desperation is rooted in fear. Some women are scared of being alone, not being able to have children, or of never finding a decent guy who won't break their heart. The prospect of any one of those scenarios strikes fear into the hearts of many woman. But there's no need to fear. One bad

breakup doesn't mean you're destined to be alone for the rest of your life. It just means that things didn't work out with that particular guy for whatever reason. You aren't a single senior citizen doomed to die alone, so there's no need for the desperate dating maneuvers.

THEIR CLOCK IS TICKING

You may be desperate because you feel like your time is running out when it comes to finding a man. In your mind, you've got a limited window of time, and maybe you're gunning to have a baby before you turn forty. Maybe you've set an imaginary wedding date in your head, planned the entire affair down to the location, flowers, and bridesmaids dresses. You've even got your own wedding dress picked out. Now all you need is the guy to marry and your perfect wedding is complete. Wouldn't it be much smarter to find the guy first and then plan the wedding?

Before desperation strikes, stop for a minute. Take it easy. Breathe. Everything is going to be all right. Ask yourself this: Is it better to be single and happy or in a relationship that isn't working just for the sake of having a guy in your life? You don't have to date desperate because, no matter what your romantic circumstances are, you're not desperate. You're a diva! And *desperation* is not a word in a diva's vocabulary.

No matter what happens, if it's part of your dating destiny, you will have a baby one day and when you do, it's going to be with a guy who is qualified to share your life with you and be the father of your child. But pulling desperate moves with an ex or any guy you date isn't the way to make it happen.

Ways Women Act Desperate

Desperation on the dating scene comes in many different forms. You don't want to partake in any of them—you're a smart, confident diva, and you don't need to resort to any of these tactics to get or keep a man.

....

3 COMMON Tactics Desperate Damsels Use and How to Avoid Them

1. **Ignoring the signs that your guy is a jerk**—even though your Built-in Bullshit Detector went off a million times, you still continue to date a guy you know is wrong for you. That's desperate!

2. **Letting a guy have a free pass to your v-jay jay**—if you let a guy use you for sex under the guise that it's a relationship, you're only fooling yourself. That's dumb and desperate! Read on to learn more about this desperate move.

3. **Wanting to get too serious, too soon**—if you've only been dating a guy for a few months and you're already dropping hints about babies and marriage, you're dating desperate. Stop it already!

> **The AVERAGE Guy**
>
> Guys aren't into desperate women. They would rather spend their time with a confident one any day of the week.

You don't have time to waste trying to be with a guy who doesn't want to be with you! If he isn't returning your calls, stop calling him. If he doesn't answer your text messages or e-mails, don't send him any more of them. By acting as though you don't exist, he is sending you a message—you're just not the one for him.

GIVING UP THE GOODS TOO SOON

Another desperate dater is the girl who has sex too quickly with a guy she's dating. She does the deed way too soon in hopes that her bedroom moves will help seal the deal for a committed relationship. That's what Paula, twenty-nine, did when she committed the cardinal sin of dating—dropping her dress for a guy before she even had a chance to check him out or get to know him. Over and over, Paula kept making this her signature dating move, hoping one of the guys she dated would stick around, but they never did. Paula's relationships only lasted a few months and after a while, she realized why.

The **AVERAGE** Guy

When you have sex with a guy on the first date, he thinks you're a slut who sleeps with every guy after just one dinner and a movie.

"I was so desperate to settle down with a guy before I was thirty and have a baby before I was thirty-five that I got it into my head that having sex with them right off the bat was the way to keep them interested," Paula says. "I was so wrong.

When you sleep with a guy too quickly, he won't respect you enough to date you long-term and he certainly won't make you his wife."

You're on your way to becoming a strong, confident diva who doesn't need to pull desperate moves like giving up your goods on the first date.

Surviving Post-Breakup Dating

Today, there are more dating options than ever before. Not only can you find love by phone or in person, but now you can do it through e-mail, websites, a webcam, and IM as well. Just as the ways you can date have changed with the evolution of technology, so have the rules, some spelled out and some simply unspoken. To help you through it, here are six rules you must memorize.

....

6 ULTIMATE Rules for Post-Breakup Dating

1. **Don't have sex unless you're in a real relationship.** That's what your rebound guy was for. You're on the official dating scene now. From here on out, if you're seeing a guy and you haven't clearly defined your relationship, do not sleep with him. Do not assume that just because you're dating, you're an exclusive couple or "in a relationship." "Men don't think like women do when it comes to sex," says the Average Guy. "To women, sex is about letting a man into their bodies and souls, but to guys it's just about the sex. So make sure the guy you

sleep with feels the same way you do *before* you sleep with him."

2. **Don't chase a guy who doesn't want you.** Promise yourself that you will only date guys who want to date you. You will not obsess about some guy who hasn't returned your call. You are not going to chase after him trying to find out why he didn't dial your digits. If he didn't call, it's because he found someone that he wants to date more than you.

> **The AVERAGE Guy**
>
> To guys, sex is just sex; it's not a sign that you are now a couple and dating each other exclusively.

3. **Don't date married men.** When you get out on the dating scene, you're going to run into a lot of married men. Most of them will tell you their tales of romantic woe, complain about their wives, or flat-out request your company as a mistress. Why would you want to play second fiddle to some guy's wife? Why would you want to be the woman a married man dates in between all the lies he tells to his wife? That's not you!

4. **Don't date a guy who's clearly undateable.** There are many things that would make a guy undateable—his hygiene, his lack of motivation, his marital status. So, if a guy you decide to date is emotionally unavailable, has anger issues, a nasty almost-ex-wife, or a dangerous drug habit, move on. You want a guy who is in touch with his feelings, can be calm, doesn't have drama with an ex, and doesn't do drugs.

5. **Don't rescue him.** Women love a hard-luck story. They always want to help. This is our motherly instinct gone horribly awry. Don't date a bad boy because you're convinced you can transform him into a family man. That's who he is and there's nothing you can do to change it, so don't waste your time trying. Also, don't give a broke guy any money. That's one of the worst things a woman can do. Remember that any guy who asks you for money to pay a bill, help a friend, or any other reason, is probably taking you for a ride. Just say no!

6. **Don't doubt him.** Men will tell you who they are and what they want almost immediately, so don't doubt it. When you meet a guy who says he hasn't had a serious relationship in five years, don't think it's because he's never met the right woman. It's because he has issues that he hasn't dealt with and that no other woman can deal with either. He may also have issues with commitment that he hasn't addressed yet. Whatever the reason, believe him when he says he hasn't been able to keep a solid relationship together in the last five years.

Though you've definitely dated losers in your past, you've probably also dated a few nice guys. And, like many before you, you've most likely done silly things to screw up that perfectly good relationship with a cool guy. Making these mistakes is called self-sabotage, akin to deliberately shooting yourself in the foot. The good news is that after reading this book, self-sabotage will be a thing of the past when your next great relationship rolls around.

What Is Self-Sabotage?

Self-sabotage is a bunch of random little acts of stupidity you initiate that turn your relationships with men upside down, taking your emotions along with it. Usually, self-sabotage hits when you realize you may actually have genuine feelings for a guy. You think you might have a future with him free of cheating, lying, or hurting, but you don't want to fall too far emotionally yet, since you've been burned in the past. So even though you don't really mean to, you screw it up. Why? You're scared and skeptical, and you want to protect yourself from what you think is the inevitable downfall of a relationship with a possible future. So with uncanny precision, you start thinking ridiculous thoughts like the guy is a player or he's too good to be true, so why bother.

After a few weeks of thinking like that, you're certain you've been wasting your time, so you behave like boy-crazy high-school girl and do things like stop answering his calls or pretending to be so busy that you never see him. Before you know it, you get exactly what you were subconsciously gunning for—your relationship is over.

That's exactly what happened to Anne, twenty-seven. She had been burned by bad boyfriends before. She spent four years with a guy she discovered was cheating on her while draining her bank account behind her back. Anne sought therapy for a few months after the breakup. She thought she was over him, but instead of moving on, she became a self-sabotager. For one silly reason or another, she sent most of the guys she dated packing by the second date.

"I certainly didn't want to be single," Anne says. "But after what I went through with my ex, I spent all my time looking out for any signs of infidelity or deception instead of enjoying the relationship." Once Anne recognized what she was doing to herself and her relationships, she was able to change her behavior. "I didn't realize what I was doing was self-sabotage," says Anne. "I also didn't recognize the effects of my behavior or why I was doing it."

Does This Sound Like You?

Which of the following random acts of stupidity have you committed in your dating past?

- **Wearing that putrid perfume called "I'm Helpless"**—guys don't like women who are a lot of work to date. They much prefer the lovely scent of a woman who is independent and in control of her life and who doesn't need to have her man at her beck and call every minute of every day. So if you think calling your new guy every time something goes wrong in your life will turn him on, think again!
- **Pretending to be someone you're not**—if you don't like football, don't lead a guy you're dating to think you do. He will only be disappointed when he finds out you can't tell a touchdown from a touchback.
- **Giving a guy a bird's-eye view of your inner bitch**—guys don't like women who treat them like dirt. Despite what you may have read in other dating advice books, men don't want to be with a bitch.

✦ **Having sex too soon**—one of the most important dating decisions you're going to make is when to have sex with a guy. If you make the wrong one, you'll regret it for life. Before you go out on the dating scene again, decide how long you're going to wait to have sex with a guy you really like. Is it after just three dates or three months into the relationship? Only you can answer that question. But remember, sex comes with commitment. Men don't equate sex with love, so they'll have it whenever they can get it, whether that's on the first date or the fifth. But they're not going to marry the girl who sleeps with them on a first date.

> **The AVERAGE Guy**
>
> Guys are always disappointed when they find out a girl they're dating isn't who she's been pretending to be.

✦ **Moving in too soon**—the second most important dating decision you're going to make is whether or not to live with a guy you're dating. You know how it is when you start dating a new guy you really like: before you know it, either he's at your place or you're at his all the time. Inevitably, the question of cohabitation comes up. Don't even think about it, though, until at least a year or two of dating him (and preferably with an engagement ring on your finger and a wedding date set!).

✦ **Acting needy**—you don't need a man in your life to be happy. But if you have one, you don't need to be with him twenty-four hours a day. Go places and do things on your own from time to time.

- **Acting like a drama queen**—guys despise drama, so for them, a woman flying off the handle for every little thing isn't attractive in the least. Instead, try to go with the flow and just let things be, even if you don't have control over everything.

- **Reliving your childhood**—just because your mom was paranoid your dad was cheating and snooped through his things or hired a private eye to catch him, doesn't mean you have to do it, too.

> **The AVERAGE Guy**
>
> Guys get used to having a live-in girlfriend and never propose because they figure— why buy the cow when you can get the milk for free?

- **Looking for a payoff from your self-sabotage**—when you act like a drama queen, have sex too soon, or act needy, ask yourself what you're getting out of that particular behavior. Are you doing it because you think you're playing hard to get? Do you think it's going to make you look really busy, popular, or important? Is the payoff you get worth the grief this behavior causes your boyfriend?

- **Keeping secrets**—granted, every girl's got secrets, but keeping them from a potential mate is a recipe for disaster. If it is something harmless, like you snore when you sleep, there's no need to reveal that right away, but if you were married before, have kids, or have a medical condition, those are all very important things that you've got to reveal.

Committing any of the aforementioned random acts of stupidity can cause a potential romance to fizzle even before it starts, so don't do it. This time around, instead of repeating the same old dating mistakes you usually do, give yourself a chance—a real shot at healing your heart and finding lasting love.

Stop the Madness

So how do you stop committing these random acts of stupidity? Here are some techniques that have worked for DontDate HimGirl.com members.

ANALYZE YOUR PAST

Examine your childhood and what you were taught about men, relationships, dating, and love. If your mom taught you men can't be trusted, you will probably be aloof and suspicious of the actions of most of the men you date. But you can't continue using that influence as an excuse. It's time to recognize it and work to conquer that obstacle. "You can overcome the deficits of your childhood by using them to understand your past and how to interact in romantic relationships today," says dating expert Kerry Gray. "There is no need to keep sabotaging yourself and your chances at finding love."

When you were young, your mother probably gave you the "Beware of Boys" speech. You know, the one where she tells you that you can never trust a guy, no matter how good he seems. If your mother had a broken heart or two by the time she had you, she'll tell you that all men lie, cheat, steal, and deceive women. There's some truth to the notion that every woman who is the offspring of a brokenhearted woman is romantically predisposed to think that most men are worthless snakes, even though that's not true.

If you had a father who made a professional career out of breaking women's hearts, particularly your mother's, you've got an excuse for not wanting to get screwed over by a man like your mother did. You don't want to end up like your mother. It's understandable, but having a jerk for a father isn't a valid excuse for denying yourself the opportunity to heal your heart and find love again.

Don't put the damage your father did to your mother on the shoulders of every guy you date. All you're really doing is branding each guy a deceitful, cheating jerk, automatically assuming he can't be trusted based on what your dad did to your mother or what one or two bastard boyfriends in your past did to you.

Katherine, thirty-two, did that with almost every guy she dated after her last breakup. "Every time I met a guy, I thought about what my father had done to my mother," says Katherine. "I wanted to make sure that I didn't get hurt, so I was suspicious of everything a guy did and I really didn't have a reason to be."

Every guy you date deserves to be taken at face value and not be automatically judged by the actions of your exes or your dad or anyone else who led you to believe all men were jerks. Remember, not every guy comes out of the womb born a cheater, liar, or loser. It's a learned behavior.

DON'T TRY TO GO BACK IN TIME

If you were having trouble with getting over your ex, I certainly hope that Steps 1–8 of this book have helped you do that.

If you're still struggling, you may find yourself self-sabotaging by continuing to try to get your ex back. Now that you're aware of the dire consequences of self-sabotage, you must learn how to avoid screwing up your chances at future romance by hoping you'll get your ex back.

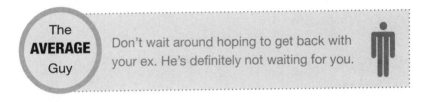

The AVERAGE Guy Don't wait around hoping to get back with your ex. He's definitely not waiting for you.

We've already discussed how trying to get back with your ex is a telltale sign of a desperate dater. Why do women do this? Some women fear being single. Still others figure since they already know their ex's bad habits, it's better to get back together with him than take the time to get to know the annoying habits of a new guy. And still other women simply feel comfortable going back to what they know rather than facing the unknown on the dating scene. So they wait and hold out hope of getting back together, thinking that things in the relationship will change. Don't be one of those women!

While you might be waiting for that reconciliation, your ex isn't. You're putting your life on hold and wasting your precious time hoping to get back together with a guy who doesn't want to get back together with you. He's already moved on, even if he says he hasn't. He's probably dating someone new right now but doesn't want you to know about it.

That's what Jane, twenty-nine, did. Let's see where that got her. "I was convinced I couldn't live without my ex. I really wanted to get back together with him," Jane says. After months

‘me waiting, Jane realized reconciliation with
...er boyfriend wasn't in the cards.

"We talked about getting back together," says Jane, "but
he was having too much fun being single." That's when Jane
decided to date smarter. "I had let so many great guys go by
while I waited to get back together with my ex," she says. "I'll
never do that again."

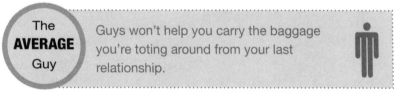

The **AVERAGE** Guy

Guys won't help you carry the baggage
you're toting around from your last
relationship.

Someday you will look back at your relationship with your ex
and this breakup and you'll ask yourself what in the world you
were thinking when you got together with him in the first place.
Your friends may tell you they tried to warn you about him, but
you wouldn't listen to them. It happens. Like many women, you
became convinced that no one knew your former boyfriend as
well as you did. But you were wrong. In reality, you didn't know
him at all. And that fact is causing you a great deal of pain.

I understand. Finding love again is possible, as long as you
don't screw up your chances at real romance!

Retrain Your Pretty Little Brain about Boyfriends

After you've been battered by love and nursed a broken heart
a few times, you start to develop certain notions about love,

dating, and guys in general. When you think about the bas-tards you've dated, you might start to think all guys are the same as your ex. But nothing could be further from the truth! Believe it or not, there are good guys out there, ones who won't cheat, don't lie, and aren't in the habit of putting you down or abusing you. They're genuinely just decent guys that any woman would be lucky to call their own.

To get one, you have to change the way you think about love, young lady! Here's how:

- Let your guard down a little bit. Do away with that tough exterior you've got and see where it leads you.
- Stop thinking every guy is a natural born bastard.
- Stop thinking you'll only let a guy get so close without commitment—because let's face it, a girl's got needs.
- Don't walk around with your emotions shut down, unable to feel love, lust, or anything for that matter. Eventually, the guy you're dating will follow your lead and do the same and just like that, with a loud thud, the relationship is over.

Retraining your brain is easier than you think, but it will take a little effort on your part. Remember that there are good guys out there and when you get one, you've got to extend your trust until he shows you he really can't be trusted. It's tough to do, but it's an integral part of the dating process. Sure, it's easier to put up a wall emotionally and leave it up at all times, but that's not going to get you the loving relationship with a guy you deserve. Sporting an impenetrable emotional wall is going to make it tougher for you to find love.

Kerry Gray advises women to "work from the belief that you can create a rewarding, loving relationship that will last and do everything you can to make that happen."

Believe that you can find love again. Believe that you deserve it and most importantly, believe that it can happen to you, because it most certainly can.

Don't be one of those women always complaining about how true love just can't happen to someone like you. Don't fret, girl! Now that you know how to avoid diminishing your chances at romance, let's talk about the ins and outs of dating the smart, DDHG way!

Is Your New Sweetheart Really Your Soul Mate?

When You Find Someone with Soul Mate Potential

Do you believe that everyone has a soul mate? Or maybe everyone has more than one? If you do believe in multiple soul mates, you're not alone. Many people from all walks of life are convinced that everyone has another person who is our other half—the perfect fit we've been searching for.

"I am one of those who believe there is more than one soul mate for each of us," says dating expert Alison James. "But if you can find even one you are doing better than most of us, because it's hard." The late singer Marvin Gaye agreed. The *Sexual Healing* singer said that "marriage is miserable unless you find the right person that is your soul mate, but that takes a lot of looking."

So if you've successfully relaunched your post-bad-boy dating career and have met a great guy, congratulations! Once you're in a serious relationship with someone who really might be "the one," you've got a whole host of exciting things to think about. Before you get ahead of yourself, check out this chapter for some key tips on how to move into forever territory!

Make Sure Your Potential Soul Mate Is Solid

The guy you're dating has probably passed your background check with flying colors, and his personality probably matches your list of criteria pretty well too. Now, it's time to check out his character. Granted, you'll never know exactly what your guy is thinking, but his actions can certainly tell you a lot about the type of person he is and how he'll treat you in a long-term relationship. Katie, thirty-one, found out a lot about her last boyfriend just by observing his actions.

"I dated this guy who I had done a background check on and he came up fine," says Katie. "But what I didn't know was that while he was dating me, he was also actively trying to date other women." Katie soon figured out that the guy she thought she was going to marry really had no integrity at all. "When I confronted him, he didn't apologize, he just made up some lame excuse for what he did, saying that my male friends made him jealous," Katie says. "So he cheated on me not just once, but many times over a long period of time and that was the moment I knew our relationship was over for good."

To find out what kind of character the man you're dating really has, observe him. "You can tell a lot about a guy by watching the way he interacts with the other people in his life," says the Average Guy. For example, how he interacts with his mother— does he make time for her? Is he kind to her? How does he act around kids? Does he take a hands-off approach or does he get in there and have fun with them? Is he environmentally conscious? Does he recycle? Does he help out his friends?

When you get positive answers to these kinds of questions, you can be even more confident in his soul mate potential.

If You're Still Starting to Doubt Him . . .

Don't! Finding a great guy is hard enough. So when you think you may have found one who could be your soul mate, remember what we talked about in Step 9—don't make silly mistakes that will end up driving him away before he's even had a chance to think about proposing to you. That's how Candace, twenty-seven, almost lost her soul mate. "I knew that I was so in love with my boyfriend," says Candace, "but then I got scared and started doubting that he was really the one. It was stupid, but I drove him crazy thinking he was too good to be true and doubting his intentions."

Luckily, Candace was able to get over her fear and later married her soul mate. Being afraid once you know that you've found the love of your life is a common mistake women make. After all, you have to protect your heart from all the losers out there! Here are nine soul mate mistakes to avoid.

....

9 SOUL Mate Mistakes to Avoid

1. **Believing he's too good to be true**—if you meet a guy who is kind, loving, doesn't lie to you, and treats you with respect, it's not an illusion. There isn't something wrong. You deserve to be loved like that and don't you ever forget it.

2. **Convincing yourself that he'll cheat eventually, so what's the point in making a solid commitment to him for life**—just because a few guys have cheated on you in the past doesn't mean the guy you're dating will. Don't treat him like he's already doing it, because if he's not, you're going to drive him away.

3. **Letting your girlfriends put him down**—you love them, but don't your girlfriends have an uncanny way of magnifying your man's flaws? If it's clear that the guy you're dating really cares about you and you know that in your heart, don't let their opinions influence how you feel. If they've got valid concerns (like he's got a drug problem), that's one thing. But if they just don't like the way he dresses or the way he styles his hair, don't let that change the way you feel about him.

4. **Being afraid**—it's okay to be afraid of the dating scene. It's a jungle of jerks, gigolos, and liars out there, but you're much better prepared to deal with them now that you're reading this book. Fear can cause you to make a critical soul mate mistake. It might get in the way and prevent you from dating a guy who could potentially be the man of your dreams. Remember, there's nothing to fear. You're a strong, smart girl who's learned a lot since reading this book. You know what to do!

5. **Having one foot in the relationship and one foot out**—if you're convinced you've found your soul mate, commit to him. Don't let him get away from you so that some other lucky girl can land him. Enjoy how great he is instead of wondering what else is out there. Put both feet in the water and see where it leads you.

6. **Not extending trust**—if you've been the victim of a bad breakup or two, it's understandable that you now have a hard time trusting the men you date. But you're going to have to work on that in order to hold on to your soul mate. If he's proven that he's trustworthy, keep him. Just because a guy broke your trust in the past, don't let that

prevent you from committing to a life with your soul mate today.

7. **Seeing your soul mate through the eyes of the baggage from your last bad relationship**—not every guy you meet is going to be like the guy who broke your heart. The awful things he did will not be the things your soul mate will do, so stop judging him as though he was your ex. If your ex came home at all hours of the night after partying with the boys five nights a week, don't judge your new boyfriend if he occasionally hangs out with his friends after work. He's not your ex and he's not doing the same things your ex did.

8. **Believing in the fairy tale**—*Cinderella* is a great work of fiction, but it isn't real. Neither is the notion that romantic relationships are perfect. Just as there are no perfect people, you won't find a relationship that doesn't have problems. The key is to solve those problems together as a team and to find solutions with your soul mate. "We all have a romantic notion of what relationships are supposed to be like but ultimately even the best relationships don't live up to this fairy-tale image," says dating expert Alison James. "Relationships have their ups and downs and they require a lot of work. Unfortunately, today people often flee at the first sign of trouble. Those who stay know that once you make it through the tough times, the relationship is even stronger."

9. **Love isn't a game, so don't treat it like one**—don't play the perilous game of *What If* that so many women play. Don't ask yourself hypothetical questions about what your soul mate would do in a given situation. All you're

doing is setting your soul mate up for a series of need-less challenges. When you do that, you're not really in a relationship that means something. You're just carefully orchestrating a bunch of tests for your guy and hoping he'll pass them. If you think he's your soul mate, you should be way past that.

"One of the worst things a woman can do is to set guys up," says Nathan, thirty-nine. "We hate it when women do things just to see what we're going to do. My ex did that when we were together and it drove me nuts." Don't set little traps for your guy for no reason—like getting another girl to hit on him just to see what he'll do. That's called entrapment.

So now you know how *not* to make silly mistakes when you find a guy who could be your soul mate. Now, let's make sure he's everything he says he is.

There Are No Guarantees

So you think your guy is for real, but how do you really know for sure? Unfortunately, you may never get the confirmation you're looking for. There are no guarantees in life and love is one of the areas of life where nothing is certain. Look out for the signs that your guy isn't who he appears to be and go with your intuition to make your final decision. That's really all you can do.

You're probably never really going to know from the begin-ning if he's really your soul mate. Right now, all signs point to you and your guy spending the rest of your lives with each other in wedded bliss. But the truth is you'll never really know. The only thing you can do right now is make an informed decision based on the research you've collected and the things you've seen from him. Any way you look at it, you're taking a chance when you commit to a guy you think might be your soul mate. After all, he could be your soul mate now, but you don't know if he's going to be in the future.

The **AVERAGE** Guy

If you've dated a guy for at least a year without him cheating on you, lying to you, or stealing from you, he might just be soul mate material.

The best thing to do when faced with the prospect of committing your life to your possible soul mate is to trust your intuition, that Built-in Bullshit Detector given to you by Mother Nature. You know in your heart whether or not the guy you're dating is going to be around for the long haul. You know because you've spent time with him, you've likely slept with him, and gone through ups and downs with him. You know what he's really about.

Now stop thinking about your sweetheart for a minute and think about your last relationship. What a jerk he was, right? Does your current soul mate act like your ex? Does he do the same awful things your ex did to you? If not, then give him a chance and see where your journey in love takes you both. But if you find the opposite, stop.

Don't worry. You're a smart girl and you've done your homework with this guy, so trust in the fact that you're prepared. Remember to base your decision about committing to your soul mate on what you know about him, not on what your bastard ex did to you.

PART 3

IF YOU'RE STILL LOOKING FOR LOVE . . .

Love Being Single

Forget about the Stigma

If you haven't found your soul mate yet, be patient. That's perfectly fine! I know you're probably tired of hearing that, but you have to accept it. Even though you may be out there on the dating scene, you're probably still picking up those last little pieces of your broken heart. Contrary to popular belief, being a single girl doesn't suck. Okay, right now maybe it sucks a little for you, but that's only because you've had your heart broken recently.

But being a singleton isn't as bad as you think it is. Being single doesn't mean you're defective or that you won't have kids. It doesn't mean that you're going to die a miserable death, abandoned and alone. But somehow, that's what many women believe about living the single life.

"Men and women both feel a desire to meet 'the one' and both express a fear that they will end up old and single living in a shoddy house with ten cats," says Alison James. "This fear of being alone forever is normal but we need to be aware of the way it can affect us. Often we stay in relationships that aren't right for us just so we can have a warm body around. Remember—it is far better to be single than to be in a bad relationship."

Have You Taken the Time to Love Being Single?

Some women drift aimlessly from one relationship to another, just so they don't have to wear the singleton stamp. These women never stop to take a breath, so they never really get the chance to see how happy they can be all by themselves. Who says you can't be single and still be happy? You most certainly can, but for some women, the thought of being without a man is a scary one. Some women need a man in their life, any man, to be content. But you weren't born with a hot guy by your side and you've made it through quite a bit of your life without a soul mate, so what's the big deal? If you can't stand to be by yourself, how can you expect a guy to stand being with you?

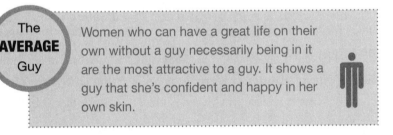

The **AVERAGE** Guy

Women who can have a great life on their own without a guy necessarily being in it are the most attractive to a guy. It shows a guy that she's confident and happy in her own skin.

Being alone doesn't have to be lonely. "Women need to learn that there is a big difference between being alone and being lonely," says Sonia Torretto. "Learn how to be alone. It's great! There are lots of positives, such as getting to determine your free time and whether you want to stay at home or go out. You also get to control the remote."

When you're single, it's a great time to work on bettering yourself in some way (at a new class or at the gym, for example), or to hang out with your girlfriends without looking at the clock (because you can only stay for a certain amount of time since your man is waiting at home for you). You can finally feel the freedom to do anything you want without having to check in with a guy. It's quite a liberating experience!

Charlene, twenty-seven, dated one guy after another who wasted her precious time. "I was a revolving door of horrible relationships," says Charlene. "It was just one jerk after another and after my last breakup I decided I needed to stop." For Charlene, being single was a positive experience. "I learned a lot about myself," she says. "You will be surprised the things you can accomplish when you're not caught up in a bad relationship with a guy."

Charlene took a break from the cheaters, liars, and losers and took a sabbatical from the tears, hurt feelings, and drama. "It was the best thing I've ever done for myself," says Charlene. "I needed that time to stop the vicious cycle I had become a part of so that I could finally stop dating jerks."

Even if you haven't necessarily been dating jerks recently, you still might not have found the perfect guy for you. Taking a break is okay! Like Charlene says, you may learn a lot about yourself when you appreciate being single.

Still not convinced that single girls rock? Need more reasons to believe that being on your own doesn't mean being alone? Here are ten more reasons that single girls are fabulous!

10 REASONS Being Single Rocks

1. **You answer to no one but you.** You can do what you want, buy what you want, go wherever you want. Being a single girl means being free of the dating dilemmas that you had to deal with when you were with your ex.

2. **You don't have to put up with your guy's annoying bad habits.** If your ex constantly left the toilet seat up, never made his bed, or had a bad habit of belching at the most inappropriate times and thinking it was funny, isn't it great that you don't have to deal with that anymore?

3. **You don't have to put up with his annoying relatives.** Enough said!

4. **You don't have the pressure of hanging out with his friends that you can't stand.** They're gone and now you're free to live life without them getting on your nerves.

5. **You don't have to deal with some guy's annoying habit of forgetting to call you if he's going to be late.** Guys have a totally different sense of time than women do. To him, having a restaurant reservation at 8:00 really means getting to the table around 9:15. Now, you can make plans to have fun with someone else and get there right on time!

6. **You can actually get some sleep for once because you don't have to put up with your ex's horrid snoring.** Don't ever underestimate the value of a good night's sleep. You need at least eight hours of it to stay beautiful and slow down the emergence of those dreaded wrinkles. Now that you're broken up, you can finally get enough sleep.

7. **You don't have to be your ex's maid anymore.** Those days are over, girl! You're now responsible for doing just

your laundry—you no longer have to handle his dirty underwear, smelly sweats, or stinky socks. That alone is so worth being single!

8. **You don't have to check in with anyone.** Now every decision you make is yours alone. You don't have to weigh the opinion of your ex, who was probably wrong about most things in your relationship. Now, you are the one in sole control of your life.

9. **You'll have more money in the bank because you don't have a guy in your life to spend it on.** Also quite worth being single for. If your guy could never seem to dress well and you ended up having to buy him all of his nice clothes, you're in luck. Now that you're no longer a couple, you can pocket that cash and spend it on yourself. The best part of all of this is you're finally rid of the gym clothes and sweatpants that he lived in every day!

10. **You can finally redecorate your house the way you really want it.** If your ex's decorating style consisted of leaving all his old, tacky things from college around the house, you're finally free to ditch the gaudy stuff and get the gorgeous things you always wanted to furnish your new living space.

Take Some Time for You

See, just because you're single doesn't mean you're a loser! That's a common misconception that plagues many women and causes them to make horrible decisions when it comes to guys and relationships. Being single is not a one-way ticket to loneliness. It's an opportunity to find the kind of relationship you want, but just haven't had yet. It's not that you couldn't find it because you're a loser; it's because relationships are complicated.

When Janet, twenty-eight, broke up with her boyfriend, she thought being single meant being a loser in love, too. "All of my girlfriends had guys in their lives," says Janet. "I was the only one who never had a date when we went out." But as Janet watched her girlfriends suffer through the betrayals, infidelities, and relationship difficulties with their boyfriends, fiancés, and husbands, she realized that being single wasn't really that bad after all.

Although she didn't have a guy to snuggle up to every night, Janet didn't have to deal with the low self-esteem that comes from finding out he was cheating on you with a coworker or the sadness that surfaces when the man you thought you couldn't live without was living a separate life as a gay man.

"Being by myself for a while gave me time to take a look at myself and what I was doing wrong in my relationships with men," says Janet. "I was able to change the things I was doing that didn't make sense and ended up finding a wonderful guy who's been my boyfriend for a while." Janet understood that being single is a chance to start over. What you were doing in your last relationship didn't work. But it's not as bad you think it is.

While you go on this journey to find love, you're officially single and there's absolutely nothing wrong with that. There are millions of single women in the world who are living great lives and doing just fine, with their hearts intact. Being single isn't a sign that you can't find or keep a good man. It's simply an indication of the fact that you haven't found the right guy for you *yet*.

Before you read this book, you had a certain pattern you followed when you dated guys. That was your bad-boyfriend addiction in full swing. Maybe you were too giving to your ex. Or maybe you were too willing to overlook the signs that something wasn't right in your relationship. Or maybe you simply trusted your ex and didn't think he would betray you until it become apparent that he had no problem doing that. But that is in the past, where it belongs. Now, you know exactly what you need to do to break that habit and hopefully, you've already started doing it. And you've got a secret weapon—your Don't Date Him, Girl list. It's going to guide you and help you avoid getting the same bad relationship breakups time and time again.

Now you know that being single isn't the dating death sentence you thought it was. So let's go about the business of giving yourself permission to have a good time while you look for a guy that is the perfect fit for you!

The
Waiting
Game

Start Fresh

In your relationship with your loser ex, you were probably very used to compromising—giving up the things you wanted to do in order to make him happy. Every relationship needs a little compromise from both partners to work, but when you overdo it, it becomes a scenario where one of you takes advantage of the other. Now, since you're single, try making a healthy compromise with yourself.

If you give yourself permission to relax enough to actually enjoy yourself while you're looking for love, you're going to have a great time on the dating scene. There's no time limit on how long it's going to take for you to find a great guy, but you can certainly enjoy the ride along the way. Yes, dating is a waiting game, but you're not going to spend your time literally waiting. To play this game, you're going to have to put some effort into it! You've got to do the opposite of what you want to do—sulk, mope, and cry over your breakup—in favor of something you should do—enjoy yourself while you search for the man of your dreams.

Have Fun!

Dating is actually supposed to be fun, you know. It's not supposed to leave you feeling anxious, fearful, and insecure as you sit across from the assorted gentlemen you'll meet over dinner (hoping one of them will marry you so your mom, your boss, and your married friends will stop bothering you about it!). Dating is a great opportunity to audition guys for the role of your next brilliant boyfriend, fabulous fiancé, or hunky husband. Short of calling guys in to your living room, asking them a series of questions, and either dismissing them or hanging on to them depending on their answers, dating is the only way you're going to be able to find a new guy to love.

So get out there and enjoy your dating life a little, will you please? Go out on dates to great restaurants, have a picnic in the park, or just hit Starbucks for a cup of coffee. While you're dating, be yourself and take things slowly. But most important, have fun and don't watch the clock. Yes, waiting for Mr. Right can be frustrating, but if you do your best to enjoy the process, I bet the time goes by a lot faster.

Relax When You're on a Date

If you've gotten tired of waiting for the right guy, you might find yourself trying to assess every new date you have to determine if he's "the one" in the first five minutes. It's okay to be excited, but don't freak out over every little thing. Don't mentally be listing all the things you don't like about him before you even sit down. Try to live in the moment and give each guy a chance. Stay positive!

"I once went on a date with a girl who just couldn't stop asking me questions," says Sam, thirty. "It was like I was on the hot seat getting grilled about every single thing I'd ever done in life. Needless to say, I never called that girl back again." It's one thing to ask some questions to get to know him, but it's another to run an FBI-type interrogation session on the poor guy. If you relax, you'll probably find that the conversation will flow normally and you'll avoid a crazy, speed-dating-type vibe.

If you're too busy taking notes (mental or physical—yes, I've heard of that!) of your date's every flaw, you're not going to enjoy yourself. Shauna learned that lesson when she started dating seriously again four months after a bad breakup.

"I just didn't want to waste time doing the whole courting thing if the guy was just going to turn out to be a dud," she says. "So I was just making mental notes about each guy I dated instead of actually having fun and enjoying the conversation, food, and my date's company." After a while, Shauna decided something had to change the way she approached her dates.

"I decided I would just get to know a guy without acting like a reporter and turning the dating into an interview," Shauna says. "After being hurt by guys so many times, I was actually able to put my fear, nervousness, and doubts aside and enjoy just being in the moment when I was on a date."

"One of the best things I did when I got back into dating was just relax," agrees Cynthia, thirty-one. "I decided I wasn't going to go around obsessing about the guys I was dating. I wasn't going to spend my time wondering what they thought of me."

Cynthia decided to just go with the flow. "I decided the best thing to do was to take things one step at a time without thinking too much about what was going to happen in the future," Cynthia says. "After all, I was just getting to know a guy, so thinking about my future with a guy was a little bit premature at that stage of the game."

Make no mistake about it—you're not going to make a connection with every guy you go out on a date with. That's just the way it is. It's another one of those facts you're just going to have to accept. But if you're relaxed, at the very least you give the guy a chance to show you what he's all about so you can make a judgment call.

Don't Take It Personally

Don't feel bad if a guy doesn't call you after what you thought was a really great date. Don't take it to heart. Guys behave this way for a variety of reasons that don't make any sense, but the bottom line is, if a guy does that to you, it's his way of saying, "you're just not the one for me." It's okay. You weren't the one for him, but the love of your life is out there. Be patient. You'll find him.

"I once dated a girl who I knew right off the bat I had no connection with," says the Average Guy. "But I went through with the entire date anyway. I even wrote down her address so I could make it look like we were going to make plans for the next day, but I never had any intention of calling her." For the Average Guy, not calling a date gets the message across without having the usual drama that men fear so much. "Sometimes if you do the right thing and call a girl to tell her you had a nice time, but you don't think there's any future there," says the Average Guy, "she's going to get upset and try to argue that with you. It's easier not to call."

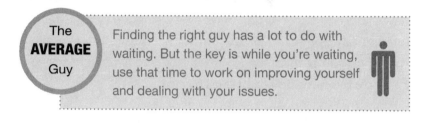

The **AVERAGE** Guy

Finding the right guy has a lot to do with waiting. But the key is while you're waiting, use that time to work on improving yourself and dealing with your issues.

So if you don't get a call back from a guy that you're hoping to hear from, brush it off and don't let it stop you from enjoying your search for love. On your journey, you'll meet some nice guys and some naughty ones. Don't let that scare you, though. You know what to do. You've banished the bad feelings you once had about yourself. You've gotten rid of the excessive baggage you were carrying emotionally and you've stopped thinking so negatively about venturing back out onto the dating scene. You can sit back and relax because with everything you've learned from this book, you are now totally prepared to handle any guy—good ones and bad—that come your way while you're dating.

Be Positive and Persistent

While you're waiting to find the right guy, it's key to maintain a positive attitude. It doesn't matter what your ex has done to you in the past. If you walk around sporting a sizable frown everywhere you go, especially on a date, guys will know that you don't really want to be dating.

Don't stay home every night because you're discouraged over a few bad dates you've had along your dating journey. There are millions of women around the world who go on bad dates and end bad relationships every single day and they've lived to talk about it. But sometimes it's difficult to stay positive when you're meeting guy after guy who isn't right for you. Here are two ways to keep your chin up:

- **Surround yourself with positive people.** If you're hanging out with a bunch of single gals who constantly bemoan their single status, it's only going to bring you down. Spend your time with friends and family who are upbeat and see the glass as half full.
- **"Restart" yourself.** When your computer acts up, you probably restart it. When you get into a funk, restart yourself! Spend an afternoon doing something guaranteed to turn your attitude around—get a mani/pedi, watch a funny movie, or whatever you like.

Don't Stop Searching

When you get back into dating on a regular basis, chances are you will have a not-so-great date or two. That's to be expected. Like many women out there, that's what happened to Carly, thirty-seven.

"After getting a divorce a few years ago, I went on some really bad dates," says Carly. "I went to a restaurant with a guy who didn't tell me he was married; I went to a coffee shop with a guy who suspected he might be gay; and I had a lunch date with a guy who lied about having a son." Sounds horrible, right? Absolutely! No single girl wants to rack up a string of dates that were so outrageous and horrific they could be featured on an episode of *Ripley's Believe or Not.*

But Carly didn't let a few bad dates get her down. "I could have really gotten discouraged after dating these terrible guys," she says, "but I realized they were the ones with the problems, not me. I recognized right away that they weren't worth my time." Instead, Carly brushed it off and moved on. So should you! "What was I going to do?" Carly asked. "Sit around and mope because I ran into a few jerks that shouldn't have been on the dating scene to start with? Not a chance!"

And you're not going to sit around and mope, either, young lady! Even when you find yourself on a date with a cheater, liar, or loser don't lose your cool. You're the one in control of your dating destiny. Your time is precious and you're not going to waste it, so instead of enduring another minute of that bad date, end it politely and don't look back. That means that you're not going to call the loser you just had a disastrous dinner with when you get lonely. And you're not going to take his calls if he tries to reach out to you in his time of need. Remember, you don't have a minute to waste with guys who aren't eligible to swim in your personal dating pool—either in cyberspace, a fancy restaurant, or the Starbucks down the block.

"Many women who use DontDateHimGirl.com and write to me are clearly wasting their time with losers," says the Average Guy. "They ask questions about men who were so obviously wrong for them, wanting to know how to fix the guy or make him act appropriately. A woman can't make a man do anything he doesn't want to do, so don't waste your time, ladies."

Don't get discouraged just because you encounter a guy who isn't honest, wants you to be his mistress, or has more cell phone numbers than he does T-shirts. It will happen, but you're never going to see these guys again, so don't let them have such a profound effect on your love life. Don't let a few jerks that weren't worth your time end your search for love.

As you've learned, the dating game is actually quite fun if you play by the rules.

....

3 RULES of the Waiting Game

1. **Work on you.** While you wait for the right guy to come along, work on you at the same time. Work on bettering yourself, resolving your issues, and figuring out what's important to you.

2. **Don't give in to grief.** You will have a few setbacks on the dating scene. You'll meet guys who don't return your calls, ditch you on dates, or forget to do something when they say they will. It's okay. Just dust yourself off and move on. Don't waste time waiting for these types of guys to get their acts together.

3. **Don't wait to date.** When you find a guy you're serious about dating, do it. Don't wait around. Take a chance and see what happens. Remember, your time is precious.

Play the Game to Win

It's important to always put yourself—your needs, your goals, and your happiness—ahead of any guy you meet. You've spent years making some guy your priority, now it's time to make *you* the number one thing in your life. You've got to stop trying to please everyone in your life but yourself. It's time to give that old, tired act a break.

"Women have this habit of acting like it's their job to make everyone around them happy," says the Average Guy. "But it's not attractive. Don't feel taken advantage of because you're trying to keep a smile on everyone's face except your own." Give yourself your undivided attention for once in your life. Make this the time that you concentrate on what you want your life to be like. Think about the guy you want in it. How are you going to achieve the plan you've created for what your romantic life is going to be like from here on out?

Use the advice from the experts in this book to figure things out as you go along. Take to heart all of the women's stories presented to you in this book—all women who shared their dating stories on DontDateHimGirl.com. Use this book to decide what you really want in a guy, what issues from your past you need to work on, and how you're going to resolve those issues before you hit the dating scene again soon.

Right now, focus on healing your heart. Guard your heart with your life and don't easily give access to it to every guy you meet, because not all of them are going to be worthy of it. Use your Don't Date Him, Girl list and recognize your bad dating patterns so you can break them quickly.

Don't forget how sexy, beautiful, and smart you are, either. It's hard not to get insecure from time to time. All women do occasionally, but this time things are going to be different. You're a great catch and you deserve a guy who is worthy of you, not one who is going to take you for granted and disrespect you. Don't settle for Mr. Right Now when your Mr. Right is out there just waiting for you to find him! With a little effort on your part, you will find him.

Get moving, girl! This is it! This is what you've been waiting for. This is the time to rid your life of the guys who once dwelled there. From here on out, guys who are cheaters, liars, and losers are officially banished from your love life forever. Because of what you've learned in this book so far, you can now spot them and get rid of them before you ever get to a second date. That skill alone is going to save you tons of time when you're out there auditioning guys to be your brand-new boyfriend.

Your dating destiny is in your hands! What happens with your heart from here is totally up to you. You are now going to make good dating decisions for once in your life. You're not going to let some guy do it for you. You're going to value yourself, because if you don't value who you are, no guy you date ever will. Remember, you are too valuable to waste your precious time with cheaters, liars, and losers. Because you've read this book and made your Don't Date Him, Girl list, you now know how to spot them, ditch them, and banish them from your life. So get your brokenhearted butt in gear and take charge of your dating destiny! There are a lot of great guys out there and now, armed with everything you've learned from this book, you can get out there and get one of them!

Good luck! If you ever need help along the way, check out *www.DontDateHimGirl.com* or shoot me a line at *Tasha@ DontDateHimGirl.com*! I, and the dating experts at DontDate HimGirl.com, are here to help you break your bad-boyfriend addiction once and for all!

Enjoying Your New Relationship

Once you've found a guy who is worthy of your love, enjoy yourself! If he doesn't match any of the negative qualities on your Don't Date Him, Girl list, you may have found a real catch. Check out these tips from the best DontDateHimGirl .com experts to develop and maintain a healthy, passionate relationship.

3 GUY-APPROVED Ways to Show Your Sweetie Some Love

You want to show your new sweetheart some love, but you're not sure how he's going to react to it. Don't worry! Here are three guy-approved ways to do it!

1. **In a restaurant, sit next to him in a booth instead of across from him.** Try to sit on his right side so you're on the inside of the booth. Lightly trace your finger up (but not too far up!) and down his thigh under the table. Do it for a little bit, then stop. He will lean in for more and probably do it right back to you. If you want to give him a

big kiss, opt for a quick kiss on the cheek instead. Go for his right cheek, which is controlled by the left side of his brain, the side for romance. Sit back and let him make the next move.

2. **In a dark movie or at a party, lightly touch the back of his neck and play with his hair.** This will give him goosebumps and he will definitely want more. When walking through a crowd, lightly put your hand on the small of his back as you follow. This says you are letting him lead you and counting on him to protect you and keep you safe.

3. **While talking face to face, slowly mirror his motions by doing the same thing.** Get your breathing into sync with his, and mimic his actions. People do this unconsciously all the time when they have a connection with someone else. By imitating it, you can create it. Just don't be too obvious. When you mirror him, he feels you have a connection, and you do, because you made it happen.

These PDAs will keep him coming back for more. You do not have to hang on his arm and insist he hold your hand and kiss you in public to make a great impression that will last. Sweet, shy, and subtle is the way to go when you are out with a new man in public.

—*Courtesy of Kerry Gray.*

CHICK STUFF That Guys Love

Guys love girl stuff. Yep, that's right. Okay, they don't love everything a girl's got, but here are three things that every woman must have because it's going to drive your guy wild:

1. **Open-toed shoes.** Guys love to see a woman with nicely manicured toes. A French manicure is the preferred, so ladies, get out there, buy some cute sandals, peep-toe heels, or other open-toed shoes and show those pretty toes off. He'll love it.

2. **Sweet-smelling hair-care products.** Guys would never use them, but they love the scent of a woman's shampoo and conditioner with fragrances like cucumber melon and strawberry. When he snuggles up close to you at night, he'll get a whiff of your delicious hair while he sleeps.

3. **Earrings.** Most guys don't wear earrings for themselves, but a sexy pair of diamond studs does it for a guy almost every time. Wearing simple earrings versus elaborate ones that weigh your ears down are the best!

—Courtesy of the Average Guy.

....

WHAT GUYS Really Think Is Hot!

DontDateHimGirl.com assembled a panel of three cool guys, along with our resident love expert the Average Guy, to find out what guys really think is sexy! Do guys prefer stilettos, heavy makeup, and pushed-up cleavage or a woman who's natural and doesn't wear a ton of makeup?

- **Richard, 36:** I know that a lot of women think that guys love big breasts and 6-inch heels, but to me, my girlfriend is the most beautiful when she's totally natural just out of the shower, without any makeup or fancy hair.

- **Adam, 41:** I agree with Richard. My wife is most attractive to me when she gets home from work, lets her hair down, and lounges on the couch with me. It's great. She's just so beautiful. I hate when she wears tons of lipstick, though. I can't kiss her too much then!

🢔 **Chris, 24:** I love girls who don't wear a lot of eye makeup. I know a lot of girls think lots of makeup is the way to go, but it's actually the opposite.

🢔 **Average Guy:** I love the occasional pair of stilettos, but overall, natural is definitely better!

Now you know, ladies!

4 COOL Ways to Bond with Your Boyfriend

Here are four ways to build a strong bond with your boyfriend right now!

1. **Ask him what he wants.** It sounds simple, but you would be surprised how many women don't go to the source to find the answer. Ask your guy what he needs from you physically, mentally, and emotionally. He will most certainly indulge you.

2. **Listen to him.** When your man is having a tough time, either at work or in his personal life, be there to support him. Helping him get through a trying time will make you closer and it's a great way to increase your bond.

3. **Practice kindness.** When you get up in the morning, commit yourself to doing something each day to make your partner's life better.

4. **Forgive and forget the little stuff.** If your partner makes a mistake during the day, don't make a big deal out of it.

Mistakes happen. Making your partner feel bad about himself is a sure way to erode your bond.

—*Courtesy of Tasha Cunningham.*

5 THINGS Your Guy Wishes You Knew about Him (But He Won't Tell You)

Guys have feelings. Really, they do! They just don't know how to express them, but that's why websites like DontDateHimGirl.com are so great! Women can find out what men are *really* thinking. What do guys want you to know about them? DontDateHimGirl.com asked our resident Average Guy to tell us. Here's what he said!

1. **We really do feel for you.** When you've had a bad day at work, gotten into a fight with your best girlfriend, or get your period at the wrong time, we do wish you felt better. But we don't really want to be burdened with having to hear about it over and over again. Why? Men don't really gossip or spend long amounts of time talking about feelings and emotions. It's just not the way we're built. Getting the minute-by-minute rundown of your bad day brings us down, too. We'll listen to it, but it would be better if you save the rants for your girls, because they can spend a long time talking to you about it and loving it.

2. **Don't ask us our opinion about what looks good on you.** Men don't have a sense of women's fashion and they really don't care. Unless you're wearing a striped shirt and polka-dotted pants to a nice dinner out with us, we really

don't care what you wear. We really do leave fashion up to you.

3. **We stare at other women walking by, but it's only because there's a woman within our view that's got a revealing outfit on.** It's just our natural instinct. We're probably not the only guy staring, either. Next time it happens when you're out with your man, check out how many other guys cast their gaze on the gawdy woman with her boobs flashing the whole restaurant. It's not attractive and we're repulsed, but we look anyway. It's the same reason people watch train wrecks like Britney Spears on television all the time.

4. **We don't think about our exes as much as you think we do.** Men have very short attention spans, so once we're in love with a new woman, the memory of the last one fades quickly. Really. We also don't usually save all the remnants of our last relationship either. We toss that stuff out to make room for the new stuff with you.

5. **We actually think about YOU all the time, but we're guys, so we're not going to call or text you every time you run across our minds.** Plus, most of the time we're thinking naughty thoughts about things we're going to do to you when we get home, but we don't tell you all the time because we don't want to seem like horny cads who can't keep it in their pants.

—*Courtesy of the Average Guy.*

Tips for Single Moms

10 Dating Tips Every Single Mother Can Use

It's difficult to be on the dating scene when you're a single mother. There are kids, exes, and other obligations that complicate a single mother's search for love. But just because you're raising your kids on your own doesn't mean you can't date and eventually find true love! Here are 10 tips to help you do just that.

1. **Educate your date.** Make sure your dates know early on what it means to be a single parent. You're not going to be able to go off on a whim, stay out too late, or be available every weekend.

2. **Don't dwell on your ex.** Talking about your ex is a surefire way to turn a potential great date into a nightmare. Guys don't want to hear about the last guy you were with. They want you be focused on them.

3. **Keep it casual.** Don't rush into steady dating too quickly. If you meet a guy you like, keep it casual. Date a few times a week and see where things go. For the sake of your kids, you have to proceed with caution.

4. **Wait awhile before your kids meet your date.** Make sure you wait six to eight months before introducing a boyfriend to your kids. You don't want your kids to meet every guy you date, only the one who's going to be your husband.

5. **Don't involve your kids.** Your kids don't need to know the details of your dating life. Date without involving your children.

6. **Check him out thoroughly.** Do a background check on each and every guy you date. Use multiple sources and be sure to check out DontDateHimGirl.com.

7. **Verify the facts.** If you find something in your background check of a date that disturbs you, verify it.

8. **Does he have a vexed ex?** What kind of relationship does your date have with his ex? If it's contentious, by dating him you're potentially involving yourself in that drama.

9. **Is he (or would he be) a good father?** Does your date have a good relationship with his kids? If not, the conflict may be an indication of what kind of guy he is.

10. **Relax.** Dating as a single mother is tough, so relax. Don't obsess about your dating life. Love will come eventually. In the meantime, be patient, breathe deeply and have fun!
    —*Courtesy of Tasha Cunningham.*

Whatever You Do, Don't Date These 5 "Nice" Guys!

Whether you're a single mom or not, you know by now to avoid the bad guys. But there are a few "nice" guys that you should pass up, too. After all, as a single mom, you definitely don't have time to waste on guys who *seem* nice but really aren't. Who are they?

1. **The Man Who Does Not Pursue You.** If a man is interested in you, he will find you, plain and simple. A man who does not call or ask you out is someone who is really not into you. Nothing ever stopped a man from reaching out for a woman he truly wants. If you call him or drop by and he is open to your company, he is a nice guy—but it does not mean he is interested in you. He can be interested in sex but not in you, so do not make that mistake, either. If a guy does not spend his time coming after you, it will be an uphill battle all the way. Don't go there!

2. **The Man Who Disappears.** We have all seen this guy. He is there and then he is not. He is available and then he is gone. He calls and shows up but then time goes by and you hear nothing from him. This man has something else going on the side, and you are an afterthought. You deserve to be the main course.

3. **The Bad Habits Guy.** If a guy smokes and you don't or you have kids, do not go on even one date. If he has three dogs and you cannot stand them, do not think you will take their place. If a guy is a big drinker and you can barely drink one glass of wine, you will never enjoy your dates and you will always wonder who he really is, Mr. Sober or Mr. Tipsy. If he is a womanizer and hits on every woman in the bar while he is with you, kick him to the curb. You will always wonder where he is and what he is doing and you are more valuable than that.

4. **The Man Who Is Not Physically Your Type.** If he is *really* not your type and you know it, move on. There must be a physical spark and some chemistry to have a long-term successful relationship. Any girl who has tried to like the short, red-haired guy when her dream man is tall, dark, and handsome, knows this is the truth. There is someone perfect for everyone. Go find him.

5. **The "Down-on-His-Luck" Man with No Job, No Home, and No Car.** Sure, you are a nice girl. Sure, you like men whether they are up or down. Sure, you are supportive. Sure, you can run fast, and that is what you must do when you meet a man like this. Run! Do not try to save him. Do not get involved with men who will drain you emotionally, physically, or financially. You are looking for a life partner, not a life project. If you really like him you can always check back later and see if the tide has turned.

Yes, these can all be nice guys and might really be worth your time, attention, and energy, but why take a chance? This is your life, your one and only life. It is not a dress rehearsal. When you spot a guy who is not for you, cut if off early rather than later. Save yourself the time and trouble and emotion it takes to end a long involvement with Mr. Wrong, and remember, Mr. Right is right around the corner!

—*Courtesy of Kerry L. Gray for DontDateHimGirl.com.*

3 Reasons Success Is the Best Revenge Against Your Ex

Do you want to get revenge on your ex? When you're a single mom who has to deal with her ex on a regular basis, that's not easy to do. Here's the way to do it right! Focus on *your own* success and make it happen! Too often after a bad breakup, women focus on hurting the guy who hurt them, instead of rejoicing in the fact that the horrible relationship is over and it's time to move on. Make a clean break from your ex and put all of your energy toward your own success.

1. **Put yourself first.** Focusing on your own success instead of revenge will make you feel better because you won't have to carry those feelings of anger and pain with you. They will be replaced by feelings of pride and accomplishment because you're keeping your eyes on your success, not getting back at him.

2. **Use your time wisely.** Second, you'll be using your time to build a future for yourself instead of wasting time dealing with your ex and his nonsense. While he's off having sex with random chicks for sport, you'll be working on creating a new life for yourself.

3. **Stay motivated.** And last, but not least, focusing on your success will keep you motivated to do your best. Plus, there's always the chance you'll run into him when you're looking fabulous and doing well. That, girls, is the best revenge of all!

—*Courtesy of Tasha Cunningham.*

Index

About the Author

Tasha Cunningham is a love and infidelity expert and the creator of DontDateHimGirl.com, one of the hottest women's websites on the Internet. Ms. Cunningham, a newspaper columnist for the *Miami Herald*, has been featured in the *New York Times*, the *Sunday Times of London*, the *Wall Street Journal*, *GQ*, *Playboy*, *Elle*, *British Vogue*, *US Weekly*, and dozens of other newspapers and magazines.

She has also appeared on *The Today Show*, CNN, MSNBC, *CBS Early Show*, Sirius, *The Rachael Ray Show*, *E! Entertainment News*, Fox News, and many other TV outlets, promoting DontDateHimGirl.com and teaching women how to avoid being cheated on and duped by a guy.